A Simple Path to
The Good Life

This book is dedicated
to the memory of my father
Sidney L. Krawitz
and to the lives and integrity of
my precious daughters
Deborah & Jessica Schaffer

I offer my deepest appreciation
to those who have believed in me
and the work throughout the years
with special thanks to
Doug Davis, Rob Dean, Jaime Aguinaldo,
Addie Macovski, Carolyn Schmith, Emily Lawrence,
Elaine Faller, Jasper Gallagher, Beba Weiss,
Fran Teller, Marcello Cruz, Elizabeth Connolly,
Ron Berman, Steve Cleere and Chris Groenevald,
my mother, Lydia May Krawitz,
and my extraordinarily talented
colleagues and friends,
Bruce Taylor Hamilton and Gloria Minarik,
without whom
this book would not have been possible.

A Simple Path to The Good Life

Discovering The Inner Bottom Line™

Olive Gallagher

Rising Moon Press
Santa Fe

Designed and produced by Bruce Taylor Hamilton
Illustrations by Johanna Becker-Black
Manufactured in the USA
10 9 8 7 6 5 4 3 2 1

www.theinnerbottomline.com

RISING MOON PRESS
7 Avenida Vista Grande, Suite 132
Santa Fe, NM
87508

ISBN 0-9749372-0-7

Table of Contents

Prologue

There is a place inside each of us where we dwell. A place where we live, exist, extol and exclaim. Where we go to be alone with ourselves to cry, laugh, swear, anguish, worry, bitch, dream, fantasize, imagine and escape. Where we bemoan our problems, decry our enemies and explore our possibilities without judgment, comment or criticism from anyone other than ourselves.

Call it your heart. Label it your soul, your spirit, center, being, gut. Whatever it is, whatever its name, it is the only totally private, unseen, singular place within us that belongs to us and us alone. And that makes it worth protecting, defending and appreciating beyond any measurable worth.

Within this priceless place lies The Inner Bottom Line.™

From the moment we're born, we have choices. Choices about what we'll do, how far we'll go, what price we'll pay to get what we want and how we'll handle whatever we get when we get it. Each of us starts out with the same basic building blocks, the same tools.

While our intelligence, instincts, intuition, senses and values may vary, we all start out possessing the same four core ethical values of honesty, fairness, respect and integrity. However, while we may stand on common ground to start, it's what we choose to do with those values that determines our standard of conduct and the path we follow.

Our ethical values are deeply influenced and shaped by what we learn from the world around us—our "family" center, our neighborhood, our culture and our environment. But while they indelibly shape our interpretation of our values and their worth, it is our choices and our personal accountability for those choices, measured on our very own Inner Bottom Line, that ultimately makes the difference in how we live our lives and what we give back to the world.

Along with our accountability, everything else in our life comes down to how we perceive, define, experience and handle power, control and fear. And what we intend. Over and over again, we will be faced with three tough questions that will keep us up at night: Who's in control? What's at stake? And what price am I paying for the life I lead today?

On The Inner Bottom Line, abuse of any kind is not respectful and therefore, is not acceptable. It will always be The Inner Bottom Line that you turn to or be forced to face as a measuring stick, a guideline, a tally to compare what you aspire to and what you've actually accomplished. That's why, in the end, the only opinion, judgment or standard that will matter will be your own.

In your heart, your soul, your mind, you will never be

able to run away from your own truth—who you are, what you're made of, and what you've done with the life you were given to live. Ultimately, the choices you make create your life.

You choose it, you own it!

Dear Reader

Please! Do NOT Purchase This Book If . . .
1. You Think That This Book Contains "The Answer."
2. You Expect It To Solve All Your Problems.
   (i.e. What to do about crazy Aunt Betsy
   and how to keep her from driving you mad.)
3. You Believe That The Mere Act Of Reading It Will Turn
   You Into A "Good" Person.

(Sooorry!)

Do Purchase This Book, However, If . . .
You Want A Simple, Practical Way To Understand How To:
1. Figure Out What You Value Most
2. Get Clear
3. Set Boundaries
4. Make Better Decisions
5. Take Better Care Of Yourself
6. Take Back Control of Your Life

OK, then, you've been forewarned.

Still want to do this? Then find a quiet moment and settle down for a while. We've got some things to talk about and some work to do together.

Introduction

Imagine this. You have no choice, no control and no say over anything that is going to happen to you and your life.

Pretty frightening, isn't it?

For too many people, that truly is their reality. Captive in regimes, dictatorships or cycles of depression, abuse, violence or addiction, it is tragically real.

For countless others, it's merely their perception of their reality. They feel helpless, out of choices or control and unable to see any way out of their abyss.

This book is for everyone and anyone who can…but doesn't know it. Yet.

Premises

The Inner Bottom Line™ is based on a number of simple premises:

1. there are only *four core ethical values*
2. everyone starts out with the *same ethical values*
3. we have *choice* every moment of our lives
4. it's *what we do* with our choices that *makes the difference*
5. everything comes down to *power, control, fear* and *intention*
6. when in *doubt*, don't
7. *abuse* is not permitted on The Inner Bottom Line
8. to find serenity, you must first find *clarity*
9. if you *manipulate*, you'll get back exactly what you don't want
10. if you're *credible*, people will believe you
11. *giving* always gets
12. doing something good when only you know what you've done is an ultimate, pure act of *integrity*
13. it's dangerous to give away the key to your private *boundary* circle

14. ultimately, we all have the same *problems*
15. when in *survival*, it's easy for our ethics to go out the window
16. *Responsible Power*™ is being accountable for the impact you have on others
17. if you don't know what you're made of, then you're not Playing With a Full Deck™
18. *power* can have a *heart*
19. everyone is a *walking world*
20. we *lie best* to ourselves

The "Good" Life

For many decades, so much of the cultural mystique surrounding the American definition of success has been summed up in the phrase "the good life." It was a popular song, a show, and the goal of many immigrants who came to America with nothing in their pockets except the dream of finding gold in the streets and unlimited opportunities.

By the fifties, it had become the catch word for the bigger home in the suburbs, the two cars in the garage, the marriages that lasted forever, and the 2.5 perfect children who did their homework and minded their parents and their manners. Every parent expected that their children would have more than they ever did. And every child took for granted that this was the American way, the good life, to which they were, of course, entitled.

By the mid-80's, the good life shifted from the suburbs to the city: the chic, 24/7, computerized, fast-paced urban existence. Symbolized by the fast track in the office, the cool pad, the hot car, the designer drugs, and the faceless, endless sex, the color of your power tie signaled to the world that you were a "player" on the move to the top.

By 2000, at the beginning of the new century, as market portfolios and mortgage rates continued to plummet, involvement in dot.com was no longer something to brag about on a resumé, and hopes of ever achieving constantly escalating incomes, owning more stuff, and retiring with stability at 65 had lost both their caché and reality, countless, disillusioned people were forced to re-evaluate what "having it all" really meant.

Did the good life ever really exist? And if so, was it really "good" or did if often turn out to be less than it was cracked up to be? When you "got" it, were you prompted to ask "is that all there is?" Perhaps what we had imagined as the good life turned out to not be that good for us after all. If there was another kind of good life, could it be more fulfilling, more lasting, more valuable? And could it be found today?

Yes. But not by acquiring things or owning the world. Each of us possesses all the tools and riches we will ever need to create and sustain our own very "good" life if we do one simple thing:

Follow the yellow brick road to The Inner Bottom Line.

Ethics . . .How & Why?

Ethics has always been one of "those" words. You know, the ones that make eyes glaze over and silence descend. Words used by lawyers, doctors, ministers or professors to articulate holier-than-thou declarations in lofty, superior voices to regular folks like you and me who are just trying to muddle through the best we can. And often feeling as if life is one big mess-up after another.

Well, all that changed for me one ordinary day. And the word has never meant the same. I tripped over the realization that ethics, if approached from a different perspective, could be an organic, universal, accessible, vital, everyday, living, breathing, simple "thing." And that it could help me make better sense of things in a 24/7, frantic world with very screwed-up values going who-knows-where. And it could even be easy! (*Not to be confused with comfortable!*)

Most of all, I saw where I fit into all of it. Where ethics fit into my life, my problems, my choices. Aha! It was definitely one of those "wow" moments. That was the piece that had been missing from the puzzle and had left me utterly cold and uninterested in rules and shoulds and mustn'ts.

For while I had always been, at best, a bit of a goody-two-shoes and had grown up with an authentic and deep respect for the law and authority, I had truthfully, despite all of my studies in religion, philosophy, and psychology, not seen a realistic connection to every-day problems except for the entrenched sense of "doing the right thing." OK. I had always gotten that. But right for whom?

I had always sensed that I had a very strong line within me that managed the choices I made with regards to honesty and fairness. And that had gotten me hung up on the petard of my own principles far too often.

It was painful for me to accept that life wasn't fair, and that people knowingly did cruel and awful things to one another. But it had never occurred to me that while I was being good to others, I was completely overlooking being good to myself. Horrors! Blasphemy! Having been brought up in a culture which taught me that being selfish was "not nice," I had never considered doing otherwise.

Now it wasn't a really dramatic moment. I didn't have an apple fall on my head. Or help create the first batch of penicillin. Or get invited to sing for the Queen or travel to the moon. (*Although a few friends have threatened to send me there on more than one occasion. The moon, I mean, not the Queen!*)

But I, like everyone else at some point, went through several life-altering crises and changes. And so, in 1985, after thirty years as a performing artist in the music business and a brutal divorce, I unexpectedly found myself trying to survive as a single, self-supporting parent stumbling through life in a somewhat weary state of mind.

My discomfort and awkwardness made me realize I needed to shortcut my way through the chaos and find a whole new approach to coping so I could set a good example for my two teenage daughters and put some positive structure into our fractured lives.

After several depressing months with a sawdust-filled brain, I did something quite unusual. I told myself the truth! I admitted what I had sensed all along and had fought with myself not to acknowledge, thus accidentally discovering one of the biggest truths of all: we lie best to ourselves!

I had a number of gut-wrenching decisions to make and in order to make good ones, I realized that I first had to define what I meant by "good." And for whom? And why?

I had always known that I had that "line" and no matter what was offered on the other side, I simply couldn't cross it.

Bobby (*a well-known manager*) found that out when he offered me a huge recording opportunity in exchange for a moment of "relaxation" on his couch and I ordered him to unlock the door so I could leave.

Joe (*another even more well-known manager*) discovered my line when I arrived in Las Vegas to learn that in exchange for a collaboration with Marvin Hamlish (*who had personally assured me that he was looking forward to the collaboration*), I would first have to prove myself by sharing my bedroom with two of Joe's henchmen! Sooorry!

I had been singing professionally since I was three. It was the passion of my life, and I never wanted to do anything else. Yet despite my complete commitment and determination, not to mention the years of persistence and endless hard work paying dues to reach my goals, there was a price constantly being demanded of me that I was utterly unwilling and unable to pay to get what I so deeply wanted.

By 1982, I had come to realize that I was a joke inside Hollywood. Me square? That didn't even touch it! I didn't do drugs and I didn't sleep around and that made me not only unpopular but laughable. However, that was just who I was, and in some hidden part of myself, I respected and liked that part of me a lot, even then. I just didn't know that then. And I didn't know that I didn't know how to be any other way.

Discovering The Inner Bottom Line™

That morning, to begin, I sat down and made a list. (*Paper and pencil with a clean working eraser—very essential tools!*) I somehow intuited that in order to figure out what I needed to do, I had to first figure out what issues needed to be addressed and solved. (*Oh, the naiveté of it all is now so overwhelming!*)

Here's what I came up with:

1. How to survive? (*Strong beginning!*)
2. How to take good care of my daughters and give them loving, steady, unwavering support during the trauma of divorce and beyond?
3. How to continue to earn a living so I could maintain the very privileged lifestyle we had enjoyed while at the

same time not neglecting the importance of being there consistently for my adolescent children? (*The old catch-22?*)

4. How to make peace with myself if the above issues meant retiring from what I had always done and loved with all of my heart and soul? (*Ouch!*) And those issues led, of course, to the be-all, end-all, catch-all, niggling, keep-me-up-at-night question.

5. How to re-define myself, my life, my purpose and my responsibilities?

That morning, sitting in the sun, the house quiet and my mind focused, I suddenly saw with clarity a simple path I could follow. It was at that singular moment that I tripped over "The Inner Bottom Line." And it was the one that belonged to me!

I discovered, totally without planning to, that private, sacred, simple place within myself where my most precious and essential values—the things that were as elemental to my survival as oxygen—resided.

I had already discovered that my children came first, no matter what. For years, I had made career decisions to turn down shows or tours in order to be there for them or some important event in their lives. And I had always intuited that I had done that, not just for them, but because that was what I needed to do for me.

I had never been able to understand how their father could miss so many precious moments while they were growing up. He had had the luxury of choice and control; he could have arranged to be there. But he had opted to be absent, and I had watched as my girls continually lost out. It was only then that I realized that for him, it obviously wasn't something that he had needed to do for himself.

Realizing all that forced me to acknowledge that I had never treated myself with the same kind of clarity and commitment I had given to others. While I had already figured out during the early months of the separation that I had lost myself and didn't even know when I had gone missing, I still had no clue yet how to begin to recover myself and repair the damage.

That morning, I found that while I had endured huge emotional hits that would take years to repair and heal, I still had the only thing that ever really counted. My Inner Bottom Line. That place way down deep inside me that housed my innermost values and beliefs. That was still there, intact and full of promise.

And I did all of this before lunch!!! What a day it was!

Needless to say, those first key issues and questions laid the groundwork for what has become my life's work, just as the stuff that makes you lose sleep and eats away at your gut endlessly defines yours.

For me, some facets remain with empty spaces still waiting to be filled, and as I continue to grow and change, I'm constantly amused to discover that as some of the empty spaces are filled, new ones open up somewhere else.

The Inner Bottom Line is a never-ending, breathing base upon which the tally of our lives is added up. It is a private refuge within which we're safe to rest and re-form. And it is a foundation of the place where you dare to make impossible dreams come true, like thanking the Academy, traveling into space, or finding the cure for cancer. And where you wrestle with your worst demons, like addiction, crime, perversion, jealousy or hatred.

So what about you? What causes you unending pressure and stress? What is the source of those demanding questions that seem without answers and just won't go away, even when you confront the seeming problem. Like Aunt Betsy, they keep coming back to visit just when you need them least, eating at your gut and keeping you awake at night.

For in the end, you will always have to confront and answer the one key question in your life: What price are you paying for the life you lead today?

In order to look at things differently, let's first look at the tools we're going to use to build a new path to clarity.

Three Little Words

Power, Control & Fear

Everything in life comes down to three little words. Power, Control and Fear.

Who's got the power? Who's in control? And who's afraid of what and why?

These words became the opening line of a fifteen page syllabus I wrote for my very first client program in 1985. What followed then poured out in a rush that completed itself in two days of feverish writing, and that treatise became the written key that opened a gate to a road without signs. A path that led to seven years of teaching and seventeen years of coaching, media appearances, magazine articles, a television series, and ultimately, a newspaper column.

And after all these years and all the tests that life continues to throw at me, there is one truth that still holds up through everything:

Life is not pretty and neat or black and white. And there will be times when stuff is coming down so heavy that you will only survive by wearing a hat. But knowing what you're made of and trusting that you can survive anything, even if you come out the other end with only your Inner Bottom Line intact, makes tomorrow a sure thing.

Good Intentions

In the beginning, I started out intending to create simple exercises and concepts to attain tangible performance and presentation results for my corporate executive clients. But within days, I realized that the content was forming itself into an accessible and unexpected philosophical statement on ethics.

I started with one simple premise: If your intentions are pure, you'll be credible. In order to be able to have others believe you, you must be clear, honest and well-intended in your actions and words. If you're credible, people will listen. And if you believe what you say, people will believe you.

In a few words, I was through the gate and down the path. Credibility. Honesty. Intentions. Trust. And those key words led the way to one of the most important words of all. Responsibility.

I've asked thousands of people over the years, during live speeches or broadcast appearances, one simple question: who likes to be manipulated? And except for an occasional unbalanced sicko, the question always gets a laugh and no one ever raises their hand!

People who are secure and comfortable with themselves don't have to try and control anyone else. They don't have to misuse their power to influence or direct you into doing or saying anything that makes you feel uncomfortable or compromised. And they take responsibility for their actions and words.

Whenever you're faced with someone who is arrogant, overbearing, controlling or hurtful, it will help to stop and consider why people have the need to behave in that manner. People who don't feel empowered, secure, considered or important often need to demean and control others around them in order to feel they're being heard, noticed or included.

In moments of passion and fantasy, however, it becomes even more difficult to sort out the real issues amidst the debris that remains. Misused control and manipulation can devastate the heart at any age. A young client, EW, found that out the hard way.

She'd been dating a young man she described as a "cool guy" for about a year. She thought they had really clicked, even though they came from very different backgrounds, and she thought he really cared for her. When he invited her to go to church and meet some of his friends, she said she'd love to. She got all dressed up and was very excited when he picked her up. As soon as they arrived at church, he began telling her to do this and that in a very bossy way. When she bowed her head to pray, he pulled her into a kneeling position and said she wasn't doing it right. EW was shocked by his behavior; he seemed so embarrassed by her. By the time she met his friends, she could barely speak and he got even more annoyed with her. The whole thing made EW very angry with herself even though she didn't know why. She thought things had been going so well. Now she felt she had spoiled everything but didn't know what had happened or understand what she had done wrong.

Isn't it fascinating how we allow ourselves to be manipulated into situations in which we are then led to believe it's all our fault and that something's wrong with us? In this case, there was nothing wrong with EW except for a serious bout of self-doubt and perhaps some confusion over what she really wanted and needed in a relationship. But the cool guy? This turkey had some major issues that needed tending that didn't involve EW at all!

No wonder she felt doubtful and undermined. Even if she had sat in the wrong pew, picked up the wrong book, sung the wrong psalm or stood up when she should have remained seated, there was absolutely no excuse or reason for this man to treat her with such unkind criticism and judgment. He apparently had issues with control and manipulation and that spelled trouble ahead in any relationship.

EW didn't spoil anything. But her current relationship with this dreamboat, despite the chemistry, didn't sound as if it would go anywhere. He appeared to care more about appearances and how she fit into his idea of the way things should be than in valuing her for who she was and for what she brought to the table.

Love and romance in our culture, especially in literature, films and media, are usually based on romantic ideals. It almost goes against the very grain of youthful exuberance to put too much rational thought into such gorgeous and overwhelming feelings as love and passion. We date, we fall in and out of love, we project onto a number of potential partners our hopes and dreams and fantasies, and then in one moment, we choose and commit our lives to someone. However, as we begin to experience them through time, we often discover that who we thought they were or needed them to be isn't who they really are at all.

This was one of those moments of truth when EW needed to ask the hard questions that had to be addressed. What was she all about? What did she value, stand for, need and want in a meaningful relationship? What did she deserve to have and feel and receive? Had she taken the time to consider what was really good for her? Did she value kindness over looks? Or compassion and humor over an expensive car?

We all have faults. But we also have unique qualities that make us special and loveable. And we have instincts and intuition. We need to use them! Given enough time, the signs of control and power and manipulation running amok will show up in any relationship. And there are always little hints that can give us valuable information about who we are and what a relationship might turn out to be, *if* we pay attention.

The problem is, in the heat of the moment, we often choose not to notice. We look the other way or write it off as unimportant. Then we end up blaming ourselves rather than our beloved and wonder how and why it all went wrong so quickly. As long as EW's concern for what others thought of her and her actions took precedence over what she thought of herself, she would continue to experience self-doubt.

She had lots of options and choices. First, she could do a personal inventory, determining just what her own Inner Bottom Line was made of and what she wanted and deserved to have in a loving relationship. She could also choose to not see Mr. Cool again, having determined that the way he treated her was disrespectful, unfair, unkind, unacceptable and not a random event.

And finally, she could begin to apply a more selective criteria to anyone she dated in the future based on a standard of values and ethics that was respectful and worthy of her. She alone had that power and that control.

You know when you're being manipulated, don't you? You may not say it out loud or even to yourself at the moment, but I'll bet a little bell goes off in your gut when someone starts to pull your chain. No one likes that feeling.

Well, that's what happens to others when what you say doesn't match what you mean. When what you say you intend doesn't reflect what you really plan to do, others will sense that something just doesn't add up, and they'll feel uneasy, even threatened. The end result will be a lack of trust in you. They won't believe you. And just that tiny speck of doubt can ruin the possibility of any relationship moving on.

Without trust, there can be no respect. And without respect, love doesn't have a prayer of surviving.

On The Inner Bottom Line, if you have good intentions, people will trust you. But in order to give that to others, you must first trust yourself.

Self-trust, like self-respect, rests upon clarity. Sorting out what and why something has upset or bothered you so much that you can't stand it any more brings clarity. Identifying options, such as living with it, fixing or changing it, or clearing it off your plate, whatever the cost, brings clarity. Once you have that, you can assess what portion of responsibility you own for the situation as well as the outcome.

And the Price Is?

So let's deal with the first hard question. What price are you paying for the life you lead today?

If you think you're not paying any price at all for anything, and that everything is perfectly balanced and nothing ever seems to upset, stress or bother you, you're either on a very heavy dose of medication (*in which case, you need to re-think how you're managing your life*) or you've found the secret to permanent, total peace of mind and need to telephone me immediately so we can write a new book together.

Chances are, if you're a normal, doing-the-best-you-can person like me, you do pay some kind of price from time to time. So, fess up. When you do have to pay, do you know exactly how much and why? Do you know how to tell yourself the truth when the price gets too high for the benefits?

Take the first worksheet entitled
"What's Keeping You Awake At Night?"™ (p. 18)
and fill it out as completely as you can.

List any situation that's causing you heartburn, loss of sleep or anxiety. How bad is it? On a scale of 0-10 with ten being the worst, evaluate its severity. Once that is determined, try to jot down what you want to achieve and find at the end of the tunnel.

Once you've finished the worksheet, you'll be more prepared to consider some specific choices and take the

What's Keeping You Awake at Night?™ Worksheet

Issue	Severity	Goal

next step on your Inner Bottom Line, because chances are, after writing down all of the things in your life you'd like to toss off a bridge, there will be one dilemma at the head of the list.

During the day, when we can distract ourselves with a number of other things, we're pretty good at pushing what's really bothering us off to the side, into a drawer or under the rug. But after hours, when the world heads towards sleep, it's not uncommon to have this dilemma pop its ugly little head up and scream.

When a situation drags on way beyond your ability to balance, cope or manage it, it's not because you lack the fortitude, intelligence or courage to do something. You just may not have found a way yet to methodically sort the issues out, surgically get to the root of the core issue, and make choices, sometimes costly or hard ones, to jettison the bloody thing once and for all, no matter what the price.

Until you know precisely what to do, what to do first, or what you really want to get out of this mess, you usually do nothing. And that's OK. Because when in doubt, don't.

But perhaps your inaction is based on the misguided or naive hope that the whole awful thing will somehow just go away, or that someone else will resolve it. Of course, in most cases, it doesn't go away and we're forced to accept the hard, cold fact that it's no one else's responsibility to resolve or fix it except ours. (*Sometimes I hate facing that fact!*)

We also avoid dealing with things because of unnamed fears. Fear of the unknown, fear of success, fear of failure, fear of loss, fear of change, etc.

Fear is a tricky component. In its most evil form, it has been used by people, such as Hitler, to seize control and take power. In its most benign form, those who understand and respect their own power retain a degree of self-control in any situation and, therefore, have little need to use fear to get what they want.

Often the real issue, our core problem, is buried under a pile of jumbled emotions, fears and complaints that has, over time, blurred its edges and fuzzed its importance, along with mounds of negative self-talk that mutilate self-esteem and confidence.

If the situation that's troubling you has been going on for a long time, chances are it's become hidden under so many layers of rubble that you may have become more upset about being upset than by this dilemma.

For instance, Kate's been in an intimate relationship for eight years that's recently become dysfunctional. Starting around the fifth year, she began to feel unappreciated and insecure because in all that time her honey, Sam, had never been able or willing to make a commitment to marriage and thus, in her mind, to her.

Since then, no matter how good things are, a little voice in Kate's mind has continued to drone on and on about this one key issue, coloring everything Sam does and says and getting in the way of her ability to be in the relationship one hundred percent.

Over time, Sam has begun to feel this slight withdrawal or hesitancy from Kate, which has caused him to pull back a little too, thus compounding the situation.

Before you begin to fill out the "Getting Down to the Bone" No. 1 worksheet with one of your own issues, let's review Kate and Sam's situation to see how this worksheet can be very useful for sorting through and clarifying issues.

First, what is the couple's current status? (*Remember . . . getting upset about being upset?*) They're both upset with one another due to a growing, confusing inability to feel as close, connected and intimate as they did during the earlier years of the relationship.

Given that, what is *the apparent issue*? A lack of closeness and an uncertainty about the depth and sincerity of each other's feelings.

What is *the underlying (core) issue*? Kate's perception that Sam lacks commitment to her that is based on supposition and not necessarily fact.

How long has this been a problem (*duration*)? Three years.

How bad is it (*severity*)? Maybe a 9–10. (*Right now, they're headed for quicksand if they don't do something positive and deal with the truth.*)

Now fill out
Getting Down to The Bone™ No. 1 (p. 23)
using the most troublesome issue you've just identified
on your What's Keeping You Awake at Night?" worksheet.

The "Bone" worksheet is designed to help you clear away debris and clarify what's really going on. Don't worry if you don't know all the answers. You will have the chance to fill out this worksheet again further into the work and compare your answers.

Getting Down To The Bone™ No. 1 Worksheet

Apparent Issue:
(Attached Emotions)

Underlying Issue:
(Attached Emotions:)

Source:

Duration:

Severity:

Options: Consequences:

Time Frame:

Solution:
(Attached Emotions:)

The Fab Four

The list of values we can choose from to enhance the quality of our lives is quite long. It includes values such as love, happiness, joy, passion, serenity, intelligence, humor, pleasure, insight, sensitivity, courtesy, consideration, spontaneity, etc.

But the list of ethical values each of us can choose from to include and honor in our actions and choices is short, for there are only four. Honesty. Integrity. Respect. Fairness.

While many other values emanate from these four, such as justice, which is determined by the judicial and balanced use of fairness, honesty and respect, these four values stand alone as the foundation for all the others.

In making ethical choices and decisions, it's rare that only one of these values is involved. They continuously remain intertwined, often one taking precedence over the others and forcing us to choose one rather than the other while making choices or finding resolution to a problem. For instance, we may have to resolve a problem by choosing respect over honesty.

Each of us has the same four core ethical values. It's what we choose to do with them that makes the difference and determines the path we follow and the worth of the life we lead.

The First: Honesty

Honesty is not the same as truth. You're either honest or you're not. It's like being pregnant. You can't be a little bit pregnant. You either are or you're not. Honesty works the same way.

In dealing with the truth, however, you can choose to tell the truth, the whole truth, and nothing but the truth, as well as a small part of the truth or even a tiny bit of it. Omission, commission, overt statements, covert hints. Lots of choices here. And lots of pitfalls.

For instance, suppose your wife buys a new dress that she's just mad about. She puts it on to show you and you absolutely hate it. You think she looks dreadful in it. Is it ethical to tell her the whole truth, hurt her feelings, and undermine not only her self-esteem but also the trust she has in her ability to make good decisions?

After all, she chose you! On the other hand, is it ethical to simply say things that aren't necessarily lies but definitely avoid blurting out the whole truth, such as "sweetheart, you look radiant wearing that dress and that makes me happy!"

Again, choices. Often really scary, hard ones. So where do you draw the line? Lying when it's used to avoid personal accountability and hurts someone else is not acceptable behavior.

For each of us, our comfort zones vary. But as long as not telling the whole truth does not hurt or compromise anyone else and does not excuse us from being completely accountable for our own actions, than it's a judgment call each of us has to make moment to moment, choice to choice.

The Inner Bottom Line starts with self-honesty. For instance, suppose a clerk gives you back a ten dollar bill for change instead of a five. He doesn't notice the mistake. What should you do and what would you do? Do you tell him? Or pocket the bill while rationalizing that "no one will ever know."

This kind of question is often answered with, "Well, of course, you should return it because sooner or later, a shortage will be noticed and taken out of his pay. Giving it back is the right thing to do." And yes, it is. Unquestionably. But while it's OK for a start, on The Inner Bottom Line, it's not good enough. That reasoning shouldn't be the sole basis for the decision.

First and foremost, before ever factoring in the impact our choices or actions may have on others, we need to consider the impact our decisions will have on ourselves!

Even if no one else ever notices a mistake was made, as long as you know it happened, can you overlook it, ignore it, keep the extra money, and be OK with yourself? If you can, your Inner Bottom Line is in trouble and needs realignment!

It's time to take the Talk Back test. Look into the mirror and see if you can tell yourself, to your face, that your behavior is totally acceptable, appropriate, fair, respectful, honest and honorable and beyond reproach. If you can, great. That's your Personal Best.™ If you can't, keep trying. Whichever it is, however, tomorrow is a new day with brand new challenges. So continue on!

One of the most daunting and yet regrettably common trilogy of issues any of us ever face concerns honesty, trust and fidelity.

Consider my client, MT, who had met a friend, PJ, for a drink and found himself embroiled in a heated conversation about Steve, a man at work who's wife had just accused him of having an affair and had thrown him out of the house.

PJ thought Steve's wife was being ridiculous and over-reactive. PJ had already told MT before that he'd fooled around himself and believed as long as no one found out, it was no big deal. MT had never been unfaithful, although he'd had a few moments when he could have. He disagreed with PJ because he thought being unfaithful undermined trust and changed things.

While MT and PJ had had this argument before, this evening it really pushed MT's buttons. He ended up walking out and wasn't even sure why. Maybe they just saw life differently now and their values had shifted, maybe he'd just finally gotten fed up with PJ's way of thinking, or maybe he was just tired or upset about something else that night. It made MT wonder if there were other ethical issues here besides right or wrong.

Boy, was MT on the right track! This is a very loaded issue and it's never just about right or wrong. While PJ and MT had probably agreed to disagree on things before, this was obviously a sensitive subject about which they were definitely not in agreement.

While a personal experience, such as someone near and dear to him who may have struggled with infidelity in the past, could have triggered MT, we don't always see anger coming and then suddenly everything can seem too much and we blow. He was only being human.

Values and ethics ultimately, over time, determine if relationships hold or fall apart. And PJ might be comfortable with his approach to this issue, having found until now that it worked for him. That was his personal choice to make. However, when someone consistently boasts and claims that everything's cool and under control, they're often hiding a wounded or insecure core that feels out of control, especially when confronted with subjects that cut too close to the truth.

This dilemma raises some key issues. What does fidelity really mean? Webster defines fidelity as "a faithful devotion or loyalty to one's duties, obligations or vows." But faithful to whom? When we make a vow, to whom are we pledging our devotion? And why? Is it out of fear of punishment or being ostracized, as in *The Scarlet Letter*, that keeps us on the straight and narrow? Or is it because we understand relationship clearly enough to appreciate how precious, fragile and critical the issue of trust is to a relationship in order for it to endure the test of time?

While there are many applications of fidelity—to friendship, to authority, to finances, even to belief or creed—that we could consider, let's stay focused on sexual fidelity. It is by far one of the most challenging to maintain and honor over time and the one that tends to be the most troublesome.

And why is that? The moment sexual tension and intimacy enter the equation, everything changes. Vulnerabilities and insecurities line up at the door and the risks increase exponentially; risks for hurt, abandonment, rejection, failure, disappointment, etc. You name it.

When PJ stated that as long as no one found out, it didn't matter, he raised perhaps the most disturbing and unhealthy aspect of this dilemma. What did he mean by "no one?" I'm guessing he meant his wife, family member, close friend or colleague. But what he completely eradicated by that statement was himself.

He would know. Obviously he didn't think he counted; that the value of what he said or did about this issue, or perhaps any other matter, had no worth. Didn't the knowledge of the trust he dishonored, or the potential hurt he might invite into the relationship that inevitably would take its toll over time in so many subtle and not-so-subtle ways?

That kind of self-disrespect can carry a very high price over time. He can shove it under the rug, toss it in the trash, or try any number of ways to ignore the truth. Ultimately, he may have to face himself in the mirror that life has a funny way of shoving in front of us when we least want to look.

Fidelity offers its truest value and substance when it's not perceived as something we give to another because we have to or because we promised we would. Fidelity holds up over time because we choose to give it. Because it's something we have to do for ourselves as well as for someone we love.

Fidelity works when built on a foundation of ethics and reflects a standard of behavior we choose to honor out of love and respect for our beloved and ourselves. The moment it becomes an obligation, it becomes a burden that for many is just too heavy to carry over the long distance.

And if we're faithful because we choose to rather than because we're bound by law to obey, it then matters if we stray. Even if no one ever finds out, we will know. Similar to the ethical value of honesty, there's no such thing as being "a little bit faithful". We're either honest or not. We're faithful or not.

For MT, by continuing to honor the vows he made and living up to a standard of conduct that he had established, he was honoring the best in himself. It said a lot about the quality of his ability to be loving and respectful, and his family was very blessed to have him in their lives.

As for PJ? He was free to make his own choices and be accountable for the outcomes. MT on the other hand, by standing on his Inner Bottom Line and reaffirming what he truly valued most, had already gained a new clarity about the quality of the friends and their values that he now wanted and deserved to have.

By invalidating the value of his own presence or knowledge, PJ reneged on his personal responsibility for his actions and words. Will PJ ultimately pay a price for this? For most of us, over time and the long haul, the cost to us in shame, guilt, stress and remorse makes the load too heavy to carry.

How heavy is your load?

Along with the importance of honesty in our own internal dialogues with ourselves as well as in our relationships, honesty is often sacrificed on the altar in a much more global, universal arena.

When our belief, our trust, our respect, even our patriotism is shaken and weakened by our country's leaders lack of credibility, integrity and choices they make on our behalf, sacred boundaries are crossed which should never be breached.

One particular gentleman's story comes to mind whenever I am reminded of the fragility and value of our respect and loyalty to our nation.

TW and his wife were having a hard time feeling excited about the approaching July 4th holiday when they came to consult with me. He was a vet from Korea and considered his service to be one of the most important things he had done in his life. While he'd always been patriotic and hadn't lost his deep belief in the Constitution, he had become more and more depressed watching the administration operate the way they had the last couple of years, especially after waging war in Iraq again.

It wasn't the first time he hadn't agreed with the way things got done, but this time it seemed to be more about values. Since 9/11, he and his wife had felt that whatever they did didn't matter anymore and were searching for a way to regain a sense of pride.

TW and his wife are not alone. Millions of Americans are struggling to find some reason for the confusion and disheartening sense of futility that has pervaded their lives, creating an underlying sense of uneasiness and anger based on the loss of the ethical issues of trust and respect rather than patriotism.

Unrest, dissent and violence are not new to our country. We've experienced great periods of distress throughout our brief history over a number of critical human and social rights issues, many of which remain unresolved or neglected today despite the desperate and important needs they reflect. Need is need. That should be enough to merit attention and resolution. Sadly, it's not.

But this loss of our government's credibility due to the discrepancies between what they have said and what they've done presents a disturbing, universal issue. Every American was touched in someway by the events of the past several years. No one is immune to the loss of boundaries we've suffered since 9/11. No one is immune to the impact our leaders' choices are having on our lives, pocketbooks and psyches.

There was a time when, no matter what, there was a deep sense that we could hold our heads up high, be proud and pull through, no matter how big the challenge or fierce the foe. Today, it's not uncommon to hear tales of ambivalence, disappointment, even embarrassment from everyday citizens who no longer feel that free-wheeling sense of prideful identity as an American.

So what could TW do? What choices did he have? How could he regain one of the most valuable things he appeared to have lost: the belief that what he did made a difference. For to lose that would be tragic.

His first option was to apply his ideas, opinions, enthusiasm and commitment to our unique freedoms of speech and choice where it really counts: at the ballot box. There has been too much voter apathy in our country in recent elections. But this dilemma goes beyond partisan issues, candidates or problems. To question whether or not he can still make a difference reflects a deep disillusionment with basic fundamentals.

Administrations will change. They always do, sooner or later. The country's moods and whims will shift, too. But nothing or no one has the right to strip him of his belief in and loyalty to the basic values he's lived his life so bravely to defend. Including him. He must not give up on himself! Or his ability to effect change and influence the course of events. Every voice counts, just as every vote counts.

The next option was to explore the opportunities in his community to become more active in candidate selection and issues. He could go to council meetings, run for office, participate on commissions or panels. There's much to be done. And he had much to offer.

Another option was to thoughtfully review his lifestyle, values and routines to see if he was in a bit of a rut. Perhaps some of his current ennui and depression could be lifted with a fresh perspective on some of the things that tended to be taken for granted.

And finally, he could choose to get involved in a non-profit or charity. Whenever we feel something's missing, we can often overcome that feeling by giving of ourselves to others. It's amazing what happens to our spirits when we get outside ourselves and give back to others who need us. We end up receiving so much more than we could ever give.

Above all, he must not lose hope. For without hope, there is no possibility. Despite how negative the current circumstances might appear, no one knows better than a veteran of a war how fortunate we all are to be Americans. And no one knew better than TW that with that privilege comes responsibility. Therefore, on every July 4th, TW must embrace hope and determine to not give up on the best that our country represents or the promise of what it can once again become.

The Second: Integrity

Integrity is the standard of behavior by which everything else is compared and measured. It's probably the most difficult and intangible value to conceptualize and sustain because the definition of the word "standard" as well as "behavior" is often culturally and socially laden with innuendo and mixed interpretation. I mean, consider the word "good." What does that really mean?

In order to answer questions like "what's the state of your integrity" or "what's it made of," let's state it more simply. Do you act from an impulse to be a "good" person with your chief goal being to show off to others how ethical you are? Does it shift, according to convenience, comfort or cost? Is it negotiable based on reward or punishment? Does your standard of conduct exist in inverse proportion to your use of or need for power? For example, the more power you have, the less integrity is present.

On The Inner Bottom Line, integrity is a fluid reflection of the levels of honesty, respect and fairness exercised in any choice and action.

Once you achieve clarity about what you value most and what price you're willing to pay to have and protect it, you will have defined your essential standard of behavior.

The issue of integrity or, should I say, the lack thereof, as well as the price that must be paid for dishonesty and irresponsible power, is clearly illustrated by the Enron scandal.

You see, I had always thought that Gordon Gecko in *Wall Street* had it right; he just didn't have it complete. Greed is good . . . for the greedy.

As for the much over-used statement, "I didn't know what was going on." Puleeze! Do these captains of industry really think the average person is that stupid? Even a child of five knows that when you're captain of the ship, it's your job to find out what's going on, even if your crew doesn't want you to know. *Mutiny on the Bounty* anyone?

Certainly the Kenneth Lays of the world today know exactly what I'm talking about. For decades, the American way hasn't been doing the right thing. It's been doing whatever you can—as long as you don't get caught! And that's not only *not OK*—it's deplorable. Disgraceful. Disgusting. Destructive. The big D's.

For in the end, our actions and choices should never depend on what anyone else thinks or knows—no matter whom they happen to be. The only person who counts when doing a tally on your value as a person is you. Earning the respect and admiration of others is a plus in our lives, but without self-respect the rest becomes hollow and meaningless.

At moments when that little bell rings in your gut, warning you that you're about to step over your Inner Bottom Line and cross some boundary into no-no land, do you pay attention to it, or ignore it, rationalizing it away? Since we lie best to ourselves, we're very clever at coming up with some explanation when, if caught, sounds plausible, even reasonable, to others.

But we still know. Deep down inside. We still know what we did, whether shorting a waiter for a dollar or cheating hundreds of thousands out of their life savings. And the price we ultimately pay in our hearts, our guts and our souls for those actions often ends up costing us more than we can bear.

That doesn't mean being responsible means being perfect. We all make mistakes. We all screw up. We make bad choices, take the wrong turn, offend others, and hurt feelings. We're human and fallible. And that's OK, even if our actions aren't. But the best part of being human is that we continue to have choices with each brand new day. No matter how badly we mess up, we can choose to do it differently when the sun comes up again.

We can do better. That's a choice. And our best can always be better. That's what growing and maturing is all about. Raising the bar. Upping the ante. And our Inner Bottom Line is our touchstone, our internal roadmap to follow and not cross, if we want to stay clean with ourselves.

For in the end, we all have the same ethics. We're all capable of respect and fairness, honesty and integrity. It's a matter of choosing to honor those values with each and every decision we make, or ignore them by sweeping them under the rug because it's inconvenient or costly to keep them on the table.

The Kenneth Lays of the world have the same ethics and ability to make choices as we do. They just think they live by a different set of rules because they have been endowed with overblown and enormous power and status. And from many recent actions, it's clear that they have chosen not to acknowledge the accountability their status has endowed them with to use that power responsibly and be accountable for the impact their actions and decisions have on those around them.

Lives have been immeasurably and tragically changed because of the selfish greed of a few. And in any society, pagan or otherwise, that is not OK with the gods that I check in with when the evening star appears.

But no matter what punishment or sentence eventually befalls these irresponsible, dishonest titans of corporate misdoing, the price they will each ultimately pay within themselves will be the most painful judgment they will have to bear. That and the public disgrace that will always taint their name.

They blew it. And despite living in a culture which sadly glorifies bad deeds, they will spend the rest of their days shackled to their Inner Bottom Lines which are in tatters. No prison in the world can hurt as much as that.

The Third: Respect

Respect rests upon honor, just as The Inner Bottom Line rests upon self-respect. You can't respect others until you respect yourself. You can't honor others unless you honor yourself.

Respect honors boundaries. Boundaries are those unseen but essential borders that separate and protect what belongs to us as sacred and separate from that which belongs to anyone else. By respecting another's boundaries and demanding respect for our own, we acknowledge the absolute need and importance of appropriate actions, thoughts and deeds in any given moment.

Respect is based upon non-judgmental, non-critical thinking and is dependent on unbiased acceptance of our own reality and the choices of others. What we believe is good for us may not be good or appropriate for anyone else. And while we may achieve clarity about what is ultimately good for ourselves, expressing opinions or telling someone else what's right or good for them, unless specifically asked to do so, is disrespectful and crosses boundaries.

For instance, consider KE, a twenty-two year old client, who was struggling with a tough dilemma. Her fiancé had just announced he intended to join the Marines in two weeks. Three of his best buddies had already gone overseas to fight in Iraq and he felt it was his duty to go, too. When they told her parents of his intentions, an argument ensued. Although they'd been engaged for a year and planned to marry next Christmas, her parents had never completely approved of him. They responded by saying that if he loved her he wouldn't leave.

Now everything seemed to be up in the air and she did-n't know what to think. Though she sometimes felt the way her parents did, she knew in her heart that he was doing what he thought was right and that made her proud. They talked endlessly, but whenever she started to cry, he said she wasn't supporting him.

For the past few days, she'd felt confused and angry. Everything seemed to be a mess and upside down and she wanted to hide until it all went away. She didn't know what to do and wondered if not wanting him to go made her a bad or selfish person.

Boy! There was a lot to sort out and handle with no easy issues. No matter how old we are, facing the prospect of being separated from someone we deeply love is over-whelming and unacceptable.

And when it's our beloved, it's unthinkable. In times of war and conflict, when everything seems turned upside down anyway and even logic seems to make little sense, it's normal and predictable to feel confused, conflicted and ambivalent. And especially so, in this situation, since her fiancé's choice to enlist appeared to leave her out of his choices.

In addition, just as they were poised to begin a thrilling new life with everything in place and the road ahead certain, life had come along and changed everything. Of course, she felt confused and angry. And out of control. She was. There was a lot at stake here and suddenly, it seemed as if everything worthwhile in her life that she had counted on and planned for was being threatened or changed. And change can be very scary.

On top of that challenge, trying to understand and cope with parental disapproval, especially about such a critical choice as a spouse, can be both disheartening and painful for any child to experience, regardless of age. The fact that her parents were not able or willing to be supportive and respectful of her choices was unfair, regrettable and tragic.

She was an adult, and as such, deserved their respect, no matter what their personal opinions or feelings might have been about the choices she was making.

Being a good parent means continually growing as our children grow and mature. To remain an effective parent of an adult child means learning how to keep our opinions to ourselves, unless asked. Letting go, even if it kills us to remain silent. At a difficult time such as this, KE needed and deserved to have their support, understanding and love.

But perhaps the most crucial issue facing her right now was one that confronts and challenges any couple as they grow through time and experiences together. It's what I call "separate togetherness." It's a tough concept to accept and an even tougher one to practice. But in a truly intimate, healthy and respectful relationship, it's a crucial part of its foundation.

It's not unusual to personalize the things our beloved does that impact us directly. In KE's situation, it's absolutely understandable that her first instinct would be to feel that his choice to "go there" rather than stay here with her meant that he didn't really love her. Or didn't love her *enough*. Or the way she wanted him to.

In any relationship, when doubts begin to surface and trust becomes more fragile, it's not uncommon for those feelings to arise. And the litany that accompanies those feelings can torment us endlessly.

Of course, there's ". . . if he loved me, how could he choose this, knowing he's risking his life and our future together?"

And of course, let's not forget ". . . how could he leave me if I'm the most important thing in his life?" Etcetera, etcetera, etcetera. Gosh, with her parents feeding that insecurity, it was a wonder her relationship was still intact.

As to whether KE was a bad person for feeling the way she did? Of course not. She was human. And very much in love and scared, as anyone would be in her circumstance.

Loving someone means respecting their right and freedom to choose what's best for them, even when it's not what we want or need them to choose, or what we think they should choose.

Instead of examining all the things that might occur if her fiancé joined the Marines and ended up fighting in the war, it seemed more helpful to focus on how he would feel if he didn't go? If he stayed at home to appease or please her. If he gave in to guilt or obligation instead of following his gut and fulfilling his sense of duty and responsibility.

How would that impact him in years to come? For anything that impacted him would ultimately impact her. Separate togetherness meant unconditionally accepting the autonomy of choice that they both possessed. Of course, it implied compromise. And consideration and accommodation. And sacrifice. It was a very fine line, and often a fluid one. And within it lay The Inner Bottom Line that belonged to each of them.

Sometimes loving someone means letting them go, in a sense, to be free to carve out their own destiny without it implying that we're not included. And it means trusting unconditionally, as difficult as that might seem at the moment, that their choosing one thing doesn't exclude or diminish utter devotion and deep love for us.

Life is not about either or. This or that. It's not black and white or pretty and neat. But in the midst of the constant chaos and turmoil, KE had been given the chance to really discover what they were both made of, what she cherished most, and the depth of respect and trust and devotion her relationship was truly built upon.

Most of all, it was a chance for her to trust herself, to stay committed and true to what she valued and respected most, and to remain constant to what she knew in her heart was best for her, not just for a year from now, but for the years yet to come.

Respect rests upon a foundation of care and consideration. It can not co-exist with abuse. Abuse of any kind is disrespectful. And self abuse is the most elemental form of disrespect.

If you don't value yourself enough to treat yourself respectfully, in thought and in deed, how can you treat anyone else respectfully? And how can you ask someone else to treat you the same?

All three issues—honor, boundaries and abuse—converge together whenever anyone crosses one of our boundaries without our permission. And layered on top of these issues are the ever-present elements of power, control and fear.

Whenever you feel in the slightest way uncomfortable, in an elevator or crowd, in an intimate setting, in a family gathering, in a legal or medical procedure, or even in a simple conversation, you can be certain that something or someone has just crossed one of your boundaries without your permission.

If you don't stand up and say, "No, this is not comfortable for me. What you've just done or said is not all right," then you allow yourself to be abused, and that, in reality, means you're abusing yourself. Saying no is never easy. It's often scary, terrifying, even unthinkable and seemingly beyond reach. But if you don't stand up for yourself, who will?

The difficulty of saying no always seems to come up at Christmas. Every year at holiday time, one predictable issue in particular prompts me to remind all of the groping, inappropriate, tie-on-one-too-many-at-the-Xmas-party people (*and you know who you are*) to cut it out!

This behavior wasn't OK when you were a kid and it sure isn't OK now! It's disrespectful, offensive, pathetic and abusive!

This past year, however, TM, a lovely soft-spoken, elegant woman who had been my client for nearly six months brought me one of worst cases of groping I'd ever dealt with before.

For more than twenty years, TM's husband had served as Senior Vice President of a large company. He loved his job and she loved her husband, which is how she found herself caught between a rock and a hard place.

For all those years, they'd had to attend the annual Christmas cocktail party at his boss's mansion. And every year, she'd endured the now predictable groping squeezes and sleazy innuendoes his boss imposed upon her.

He never did it when her husband or his wife were around, of course, but somehow he always managed to find a way to trap her in a hallway or get her alone in a corner and whisper things in her ear while standing too close or rubbing against her.

She'd tried laughing it off, making jokes about it, everything she knew how. But this year, she was finding herself so on edge just thinking about having to go through it again that she'd been short with the kids and irritable with her honey.

TM didn't like to confront people in general, and the thought of doing anything that might impact her husband's job terrified her. When we spoke, she didn't know what to do.

She didn't want her husband to be angry with her and she didn't want to seem like a crybaby. She was, of course, questioning herself and her worth, wondering if she was making a big deal out of nothing. One girlfriend had told her to just grow up and get over it; that at her age she should be flattered when any man made sexual overtures to her.

Boy, what a crock her "friend" dumped on her. And what a loaded issue. It's the kind of dilemma that makes me want to silently scream upon first hearing. Or take up sparring. But of course, I don't. (*Scream that is. Until I'm alone in my padded room!*)

After assuring TM that she was NOT a cry-baby (*See? There's that old "I'm-to-blame-for-everything" syndrome again.*), and that she might want to rethink any so-called "friend" who would give her such warped advise, we zoned in on the key issue. The dilemma was not about making her husband angry or offending his immoral excuse of a boss, but rather about demanding respect for herself and setting appropriate boundaries.

Thousands of people, many women like TM, find themselves in this compromising position, especially during holiday time.

It's a period fraught with opportunities for people to over-drink and misbehave using the excuse that "they didn't know what they were doing," which is just another cowardly way of feigning irresponsibility or unaccountability for a reprehensible misuse of power, control and fear.

We all have choices. But having choices means facing the possibility that something may change as a consequence of our actions and that subsequently, we must take responsibility for those results.

The real issue at stake was TM's self-respect. She was being sexually harassed, which is illegal. Her Inner Bottom Line was being crossed within an almost incestuous situation but until now she'd said nothing to anyone.

This man knew what he was doing. He knew she was fiercely loyal to her husband. He also knew her husband was loyal to him. And he probably assumed that she hadn't dared say anything for fear of rocking the boat. He had the perfect victim in her, didn't he?

Men like this tend to be bullies throughout their lives, but are often the worst cowards and the most insecure, unhappy guys who only feel empowered when demeaning others.

Well, this dilemma had pushed TM to the edge of her Inner Bottom Line. She was faced with a moment of choice during which she could choose to stand up for herself and not permit this abuse to continue. Or not.

And her options? She could tell her husband. If he loved her and valued her, he might stand up for his wife, confront his boss himself and tell him never to bother her again. But he might choose to do nothing or act in a way that wouldn't bring TM the resolution she needed. In which case, she might be catapulted into a whole new circumstance layered with huge issues even more frightening.

Or. She could choose to stand up for herself. Confront this bully on her own terms. As scary as it seemed, she could simply say no. No explanation, no excuses. Just no! Don't do it again! And give him a choice to either treat her with the respect she deserved and demanded, or she'd tell not only her husband but his wife.

TM was at breakpoint. It was either stand up, take control and demand that she receive the respect she deserved, or allow someone to disrespect and abuse her in silence.

Whether confronting a boss, a family member or a spouse, victims of abuse struggle with the most extreme forms of fear, shame and unworthiness.

Finding the courage to break the cycle of abuse and violence is one of the most extraordinarily overwhelming, courageous and difficult challenges the human soul can ever encounter, endeavor and overcome.

For anyone still caught in the cycle, hold on, take heart and try to trust, more and more each day, that you are not alone, that there are people who can help you, that you truly can have control and choice in your life, and that you can be free. For you deserve to be treated with respect and love.

For those of you who have found a way to break free and take control of your life, you have my abiding respect and admiration for your amazing strength, courage, and will.

The Fourth: Fairness

Do you weigh both sides of things, both perspectives, all possible outcomes and consider the consequences to yourself and others before you think, speak or act?

Are you fair to yourself, much less others? Do you have a definition of what fair means in your world? And do you measure yourself against that on a daily basis, much like you measure your level of integrity, honesty and respect upon which your actions and motives are based? Or do you change or amend the rules depending on mood and circumstance for your own convenience or advantage?

I know. Lots of questions, huh? And like most of us, the answer to most of them is probably, "no, not all of the time." And chances are, the answers are not always comfortable ones, either.

Ethics are not supposed to make you comfortable. They're supposed to challenge you. Make you reach for more inside yourself. Motivate you to better your Personal Best of yesterday.

And it's not possible or human to expect that we will either have all the answers or be able to uphold our standard of integrity all the time, every minute of every day, in every circumstance. That demands perfection and that is not ours to possess.

If so, then what? What matters is the constant, unending effort, thought and struggle to try to do it, to achieve it, and to uphold it the very best we can in any given moment on any given day.

And, believe me, there will be days when we will be tested by life beyond our wildest imaginations or fears.

Having barely endured a tragic and horrific drama within my own immediate family when my father died in 2001, I was particularly sensitive to LR's dilemma when she came to me for help.

Since her mother had died two years ago, LR had handled a difficult family situation alone. She had two sisters,

41 and 40, who were ten years older than LR and very close to one another. As the youngest and only daughter who lived locally, caring for her dad who was now in an assisted living facility had fallen upon her.

Since her siblings had visited only three times since their mother had died, LR felt very alone. Her sisters rarely called their dad and wouldn't talk about his problems because "it upset them to see him like this."

Lately, LR had been feeling a mounting anger whenever they visited because they ended each visit by handing her a list of things they weren't happy with or wanted changed. Yet whenever she told them she resented this, they'd blow it off with, "well, do whatever you think is best then!"

LR wasn't quite sure what bothered her most, she just knew she was angry and resentful all the time and for some reason, afraid. She didn't quite know what was going on or where and how to start sorting things out.

Many of us today are finding ourselves an involuntary but chosen member of "the sandwich generation," the invaluable caretakers of our parents' generation. It's a tough job for which none of us have been trained or prepared.

What makes it even harder are the all-too-common and hurtful rifts that occur among family members who are faced with taking on the day-to-day aspects of this challenging role.

Before attempting to sort out the issues produced from dealing with others, LR first needed to acknowledge and respect all that she had endured herself.

She had lost her mother. That's a huge loss that inundates most children with enormous grief and often anger.

Next, her father was no longer capable of taking care of himself and needed help. The man who had been her first role model of sustenance and protection was no longer there. The roles were now reversed. She was the parent and he was the child. Another huge loss.

Additionally, she was the youngest child; the one traditionally expected to follow examples set by the older ones. But the example being set for her by her older siblings was bereft of integrity, rationale and respect.

And finally, she was on her own, the only child willingly available to deal with the every-day demands and decisions regarding her father's needs. That's a lot for anyone to handle. No wonder she felt anger and resentment as well as fear.

While it wasn't difficult to understand how these circumstances could produce anger and resentment, fear is a more complex emotion to explicate.

Fear is present whenever power and control are at play, which is usually always. And since power and control exact high prices upon us whenever we're handed the burden of solitary and tough decisions, the resulting emotions can be ambivalent and confusing.

Since LR felt confident she could make good decisions, it was understandable that she didn't want to give up control to those who had shown through lack of interest that they weren't willing to be responsible for the day-to-day concerns.

She also knew that if she made the wrong decisions, she'd be held accountable. Those so quick to judge her would be free to walk away while blaming her for any outcomes they didn't want to own.

Her sisters' criticisms, offered up at the end not the start of their trips, were cheap shots at best. And their off-handed "well, do whatever you want" was irresponsible and manipulative behavior at its worst.

The impact of the ethics—or lack of them—in this situation was significant. Her sisters' actions lacked integrity and were blatantly unfair and disrespectful of LR and her father. But despite all that was hurtful or upsetting in this situation, she was stuck with it for the moment.

So what could she do? What could she change or let go of? What was she going to have to accept and live with? And would there be a price to do so?

She had options. For instance, she could move away. Or she could simply say, "I've had enough; you girls take over."

However, from all that she'd said, it didn't sound like either of these were options she was considering right now.

LR needed to be reminded of one key thing and encouraged to not lose sight of it no matter how critical or hurtful her sisters' actions became: she always had choices. She could start by taking back control of what she could control in her life and acknowledge that she had choices, even if there was a price attached.

Next, she could accept the realities. She probably would continue to shoulder these responsibilities alone. It would help to let go of the blame and anger directed at her sisters. It was a waste of her precious time and energy. She could, rather, focus on appreciating the compassion and patience she'd discovered within herself that had allowed her to give so unselfishly.

Her sisters would have to deal with their own stuff down the road, for it would inevitably catch up to them sooner or later. The upside was, her situation could've been worse. Her sisters could have been there all the time fighting over who decided what and that could have been a major nightmare walking.

While she might have chosen to confront, make demands or try to change their attitudes or involvement, it's doubtful those efforts would have resulted in any real relief or shift in the situation.

Becoming more detached from their actions so that she was not triggered into anger or resentment could provide her with a much needed and deserved sense of release and peace of mind.

Finally, she could choose to stay focused on her own respectful, fair and honorable efforts. For as hard as that was to do, she didn't have to take things personally; she could choose to listen to what they had to say and let it roll off her. And she could follow their advice: do whatever she thought was best!

She was standing on her Inner Bottom Line and had much to be proud of during this difficult moment in her life. In his heart, her father knew who was there for him and who wasn't. She didn't have to do or say a thing, but just continue to honor the best in her while taking good care of him.

Taking Inventory

Before we move on to accountability and Responsible Power, let's take stock of where we are on this simple path for a moment and acquire several more building blocks.

You now know that you have four core ethical values. You also know the importance of managing power, control and fear in a well-intended, responsible manner without manipulation or questionable motives in order to be credible, gain and sustain trust, and honor your values. However, now it's time to put this awareness into action.

To do that respectfully, it's essential to understand the remaining components of The Inner Bottom Line: personal inventory and boundaries. Knowing what you're made of, and knowing how to take care of what you're made of.

Before you can take care of yourself, you need to be clear about what you're made of and what you value most. Only after you learn what Playing with a Full Deck™ means will you be able to take responsibility for the impact you have on the world around you.

So how do you do that? And did I say inventory? You bet I did.

Just like Barneys or Nordstrom take inventory every quarter to determine what goods have sold and what's still left, you need to take your own personal inventory regularly in order to know what you've got on hand and what you don't. It's your responsibility, and yours alone, to make sure you're stocked up and ready to go whenever life calls on you to deliver.

You learn new things everyday. Every moment brings change. Change is one of the few constants in life you can count on. But with change comes new ideas, new perspectives, and new boundaries.

If you don't acknowledge, understand, accept and use the new things you've learned, you aren't operating at your full potential; your Personal Best.

In order to be accountable, make good choices and continually master and utilize this potential, you must first decide who you are, what you stand for, and what kind of person you want to be.

At the end of their life, no one ever said, "Boy, I wish I'd spent another day in the office!" But have many wished they had spent more time with their loved ones or been more compassionate and generous of heart? You bet they have!

So what about you? At the end of your life, about what do you want to be able to look back and feel proud? And how do you want to be remembered? As a person who earned all those millions but never gave a damn about anyone else? Or as someone who respected themselves and others and set an example of "power with a heart?"

What do you really care about? What can you not live without? What is not negotiable? What will you work, sacrifice, struggle, starve, compromise, even die for to get? Ultimately, what price are you willing to pay to have it and keep it? And how will you know and what will you do when that price starts to become too high to pay?

Taking a personal inventory is a fun, unique and fascinating journey of re-evaluation that helps you clarify what you cherish and believe in most. What values and ethics you will stand by, protect and not abandon, no matter what. For each of us, the list will be unique. But one thing is certain. In the end, it will be short.

Values

It's a funny thing about values. Like many essential things, we often don't know that something is truly important until it's compromised or questioned.

We sometimes discover how precious honesty is only when we are severely deceived. We only realize how invaluable respect is when we are insultingly humiliated and unfairly judged. We don't realize how patriotic we are until our country comes under fire.

In order to know what you're made of, you need to first give some thought to what really matters. For what counts now is probably quite different from what mattered to you ten or twenty years ago. And the inner image you carry of yourself and the way you want to be known and thought of by yourself and others has probably shifted, too, along with the years.

Change brings endless and infinite possibility that can challenge not only our own present circumstances but also that of our relationships. And embedded in that potential is the possibility that we'll grow apart rather than together, thus destroying the status quo.

That's what happened to K and her marriage. She had been married for thirty years to a man who had started with nothing and built a huge company. In describing him to me, she recalled fondly that in the early years, he had been generous, happy and full of energy and idealism. He cared passionately about making a difference and doing the right thing as much as she did.

During the last fifteen years, with the company's huge success, they had become very wealthy. They owned several homes, their own plane, and could do whatever they wanted. While K deeply appreciated what they had, she still believed, as he once had, that it was still very important to share with those who had less.

Every year, at least once a month, he had received an award from an endowment the company made. But during the last six months, his behavior seemed to have changed, and he'd begun to continually complain that it was a major nuisance to even have to go to the ceremonies.

Driving home from one of these dinners a few weeks ago, he had started ranting on about how stupid people were to think he had ever given them money because he believed in their causes. K was absolutely shocked at how derisive he sounded. When she told him so, he told her not to be stupid! That it was good business and not her concern.

Then last week, when K suggested that they didn't need to buy another property he was considering, he got nasty, something he'd never done before. He said it was his money and that he could use it and the company any way he wanted. That she should just shut up and enjoy everything he gave her.

Well, that did it! K was so hurt and angry she couldn't think straight. She couldn't understand what could have happened to this man or to her? While she had always felt that she had everything, at that moment she felt as if she had nothing and didn't feel very good about her life or herself.

Some hard truths and a fresh perspective were needed in order to sort these issues out.

Over thirty years, a lot of things can change. Not only physical attributes, but attitudes, perspectives, ideas and intentions.

Idealism is often associated with youth. Supposedly, when we're still untainted and naive, it's easier to believe in values and ethics and in making a difference. That once we get out in the world and learn the ropes, our idealism will tarnish and reality will show us that while it's nice to want to do good things for others, it's a dog-eat-dog world and we have to fend for ourselves. Let somebody else worry about those in need.

Of all the things that change as we develop and mature, perhaps intention is the one component in the mix that's most overlooked.

We know our bodies will change, even though most of us fight it all the way to the floor. We expect our attitudes and values to adjust as responsibilities change, roles emerge and goals shift. But how often do any of us take time to ponder what our intentions were and have become? Too few, I fear.

Many things could have caused her husband's attitudes, moods and values to change. And only he could speak for himself. It's possible, as the years flew by and his roles and responsibilities expanded and grew, that he lost touch with himself and the feelings that used to matter most.

But his anger and erratic behavior suggested unhappiness and pain, perhaps with himself, or perhaps in response to the reality and approach of aging, a fear of losing control, or even a distorted and overblown sense of power and importance.

Being responsible with power takes vigilance, commitment and clarity. It's so tempting to get caught up in egocentric entitlement and begin to believe you really are your success and money and position.

People with power, once they reach the "top" and seem to have it all, often suffer from the Imposter Syndrome which foments feelings of being a fraud and not really deserving of the applause. Getting "there" is not always what it's cracked up to be.

But where did this leave K? What about her feelings of having everything but nothing? Was that in fact, what she had ended up with?

She had herself. From her comments, it was obvious that she was astute, intuitive, strong, and intelligent. That was a good start. So what could she do with this stressful situation in which she found herself snagged?

First, she could remember that she always had choices. Next, she could acknowledge that she had power, control and freedom in her life to access unlimited resources and money. She could afford to take a break to ask the hard questions that needed answers if she was going to sort this out and move forward. And she should take as much time as she needed, possibly alone and away from the problem, to quiet the din.

And there were some questions to consider. What did she mean by everything? And more importantly, what did she mean by nothing? Did she still deeply love her husband? Did they still share the same values that brought them together at the beginning? Or was she staying because of the familiarity of the routine and relationship and the financial security she had?

What did she need and deserve in a relationship to feel satisfied, fulfilled and comfortable? And what values must comprise the central core of any relationship for her to feel respected and happy while still honoring her own sense of responsibility and integrity?

At the heart of all of this was the ethical issue of respect. What lay on The Inner Bottom Line was the question of whether or not she still respected this man and the values and ethics he no longer appeared to genuinely honor with his words and deeds. For love without respect doesn't stand a chance.

She may have money and physical luxury, but for the moment, she was experiencing an impoverishment of the heart and soul. And that's a high price to pay for the life she was leading.

K had lots of options. She could try to talk to him. See if he'd listen. Ask him if he'd be willing to do couples counseling. If he was willing to work on these issues, that would at least offer her one authentic avenue to finding out if they could get back on track together or if they were now traveling towards two different destinations that didn't converge.

At the same time, she could take an adventurous trip of self-discovery on which she might meet herself along the way. It's a journey we need to make regularly. Unfortunately, we usually wait until crisis or heartbreak sends us scurrying about.

Whatever choices she made, she could be assured that the answers would lie in the questions she had the courage to ask.

It's not unusual to hear about a problem such as this and react with "Oh, what's the big deal? Isn't she being a bit over-reactive? After being married to this guy for all those years, she should have just let it go and written it off to him having a bad stretch."

It's a moot point whether or not one thinks that she should or could have overlooked her husband's behavior and written it off to a bad day, his spleen misbehaving, or the stars being out of alignment. The key issue in this situation is whether or not a basic and essential level of responsibility and respect is present and being honored.

Whatever comes out of your mouth, bad day or not, you're responsible for the impact it has on others and the consequences from that behavior.

Her feelings and her concerns were authentic and real and, thus, demanded respect. To have pooh-poohed them as unimportant, over-reactive, intolerant or not necessary would have invalidated her feelings, opinions and values and become a subtle but devastating form of abuse and disrespect.

Thus, once again, through K's painful experience, we are reminded of how basic and necessary attaining clarity about what you value most is in order to take good care of yourself.

Please review the
Personal Best Values List. ™ (pp. 68–69)

This is a partial list of values for you to consider and to use as a handy reference as you begin to update your personal inventory. You may add to it as you choose.

Do you see aspects of yourself or the person you hope to become on this list? Take a moment and look through these possibilities. You will find it a very useful and necessary resource to consult as we prepare to move on to Playing With a Full Deck™.

Personal Best Values List™

Here is a list of some of the values you can choose to emulate and aspire to reflect through your standard of conduct. One of the definitions found for the word *value* in *Webster's*

joy	passion	health	fear
happiness	serenity	excitement	jealousy
love	power	courage	suspicion
peace	intelligence	thoroughness	insecurity
inspiration	hope	solitude	shallowness
anticipation	stimulation	piety	abrasiveness
lust	naiveté	sorrow	moodiness
purity	faith	complexity	secretiveness
steadfastness	stubbornness	intensity	dishonesty
commitment	belief	respect	dissatisfaction
fairness	integrity	honesty	despair
insight	patriotism	conviction	prejudice
slowness	compulsivity	humor	manipulation
loyalty	fidelity	charity	blame
generosity	clarity	verbosity	dishonesty
patience	musicality	creativity	cruelty
persistence	dignity	daring	bestiality
ability	concentration	agreeableness	shame
tolerance	motivation	satisfaction	regret
open-mindedness	energy	control	wickedness

Dictionary, is "that quality of a thing according to which it is thought of as being more or less desirable, useful, estimable, important, etc.; worth or the degree of worth."

neatness	cleanliness	meticulousness	shiftiness
organization	flexibility	mirth	infidelity
holiness	optimism	fulfillment	idolatry
hunger	exhilaration	vitality	emptiness
humanity	kindness	fortitude	anger
compassion	tenderness	civility	rage
gentility	consideration	thoughtfulness	vindictiveness
cheerfulness	moderation	choice	heartlessness
imagination	reliability	consistency	peevishness
constancy	balance	gentleness	childishness
courtesy	politeness	frivolity	selfishness
frugality	reasonableness	justice	deception
evenness	acceptance	maturity	discontent
ripeness	mellowness	lushness	evil
solemnity	innocence	directness	flightiness
credibility	magnetism	persuasiveness	immorality
perception	intuition	sacredness	immodesty
charm	goodness	sweetness	perversity
enthusiasm	morality	humility	dedadence
elegance	foresight	curiosity	dullness

Playing with a Full Deck

On our own Inner Bottom Line, within our private Boundary Circle, there exists a place where the things we value and cherish most are stored.

The Key to Accountability

It is our sole responsibility to take care of this special place. And we can call this place by whatever name feels comfortable. Special place, storeroom, stockroom, pantry; it's our choice to make. It comes with a key that's marked "Do Not Duplicate." This is the same key we'll be reading about in the next chapter on Boundaries that unlocks the door to your private Boundary Circle.

While we may lend this key to someone we trust or love, we should never duplicate it, for in making a duplicate key and giving it away, we tend to do so with the unspoken expectation that our partner will take care of us and rescue us if we need saving. (*Oh, heavens, are you still waiting for that to happen?*)

By assigning the responsibility to keep our special place stocked up to someone else with the assumption that it's their job (*if they really, truly love us*) to take care of us, we not only give away a portion of our own power and control, but we place a huge burden of unrealistic and inappropriate demands upon that relationship as well as on our partner. And that can ultimately lead to disappointment.

Uh,uh. Sorry. That's not how it works. It's our job, and ours alone, to make sure that we have the inventory we need for those moments when life challenges, oppresses and tests us.

If we don't stock up for that rainy day; if we don't keep the shelves full and ready, we'll find out, much too late when we really need something badly, that we're running on empty and we're out of what we suddenly and desperately need in order to survive a moment of crisis.

When our shelves are organized and stocked, then we're Playing with a Full Deck. Stacking the odds in our favor. And taking full responsibility for our willingness and ability to face and deal with life as it comes. For it will come at us, ready or not.

Each of us, with our ongoing, infinite choices, have special places stocked with inventories that are unique and ours alone. Each one looks and feels differently than any other, just like the recesses of our minds and hearts and souls.

So let's take a tour of your special place and determine what the state of your inventory is right now. If you don't have a special place, we'll create it from scratch. If you already do have one, then perhaps it's time for some improvements or reorganization.

Your Special Place

We all have our own individual sense of order. Some of us need to have things neatly lined up and arranged, while others can function amidst enormous clutter and chaos. Personally, I can't think unless things are neat and straightened on my desk, almost to a fault.

My father, an immensely brilliant and successful attorney, was very methodical, yet worked at a huge desk with sky-high piles of files and papers. A well-worn joke among his staff was that if they straightened things up he'd never find them again. I can assure you that he knew where each and every paper and file could be found and woe to anyone who touched anything!

As I observed and helped thousands of people over the years explore the value of Playing with A Full Deck, I came to realize that for some of us, having a room with lots of cubby holes, drawers, boxes and containers was essential, where for others, open shelving with things stacked anywhere there was an empty space worked just fine.

I also discovered while observing my clients struggling to draw their custom rooms from scratch, with styles as diverse as high tech lofts and Tuscany farmhouses to early

American or antique-filled decors, that even though the exercise was fun, challenging and surprising, it helped to initially jumpstart the process by providing a template of one specific place until the concept was mastered.

Once you've mastered Playing with a Full Deck, you'll be ready to decide what you want your special place to be. How it looks and feels and is arranged. And while the whole sense of importance in discovering your own unique style may seem, at first, to be silly, even frivolous, you may discover, as I once did quite by accident with one of my CEO clients, that this advanced part of the exercise can be fascinatingly revealing and freeing.

This gentleman was a highly successful, powerful CEO of a major publicly-traded company. His offices occupied the penthouse suite at the top of a skyscraper in New York that had drop-dead views of the entire city.

The floors were exposed stone with ultra-severe shiny surfaces on the walls and the furniture was steel and glass. There were a few sleek leather chairs that dotted the huge space and the overall effect to my eye was efficient, chic and very cold.

His desk, a huge slab of stone resting on steel legs, remained quite empty and neat throughout the days that we worked and was dominated by an enormous high-tech console that was the control center for the entire corporate network.

The work went very well the first three days. He had a great sense of humor and was quite serious about examining his ethics, his personal style of communicating and his current use of power. Refreshing to say the least!

When we started working on Playing with a Full Deck worksheet and exploring the reorganization of his storeroom, an odd thing occurred.

I remember that he was working at his desk, designing his storeroom on a blank piece of paper. It was very quiet, the phones had been turned off, and I was gazing out the west windows at the beautiful panoramic view.

He suddenly swore, quite clearly, in a gadzooks kind of way, and stood up. I was stunned, having no idea what had just happened. He began pacing back and forth across the huge carpet, seemingly very excited rather than upset. I decided to remain silent and watch, waiting until he presented me with something appropriate to which I could respond.

He eventually turned back to his desk and sat down, staring thoughtfully out the window. At least ten minutes passed before he spoke. "That's it," he said simply, looking at me and smiling broadly. "You did it! That's what's been bothering me!"

By now, I was completely nonplussed. So I waited, saying nothing, having no idea what I had done and somewhat reluctant to find out. (*Silence is always the safest thing at a time like this, especially when you're me, the inventor of foot-in-mouth disease!)*

He picked up the receiver and asked his assistant to step into the office. When she appeared, he asked her to please telephone the designer who had apparently decorated his offices several years ago and to ask her to please come in to meet with he and I first thing the next morning. (*Now, he had my absolute attention. What were we going to do?*)

Then he turned to me and said, "I owe you a great big thank you! I've felt penned up and trapped for two years in this cold, metal box and I never could figure out, after all the money we spent, why it didn't feel like a productive, creative place to work and think! Redoing my storeroom with you just made me see in a matter of minutes that I'm really just an antique furniture, old carpet, wood surfaces, like-my-comfort kind of guy. I can't thank you enough!" (*Wow! That was a good day.*)

> *Please take some time now to examine*
> *and explore all the nooks and crannies in the*
> *Playing with a Full Deck™ No. 1 worksheet.*
> (pp. 76-77)

This illustration features drawers, shelves, containers and objects that have already been labeled with values.

Playing with a Full Deck™ No. 1 Worksheet

Once you've decided what values and qualities you want and need to store in your special place, you will be ready to fill in the No. 2 worksheet (on pp. 80–81), using the Values List as a helpful reference to label each container accordingly with those values that you absolutely must have on hand to cope, function and thrive in the world.

However, when you've finished labeling your inventory, your job is not over. In fact, it's just begun. For once the values are chosen, it will be your task to stock up, protect and use them when appropriate and needed.

It will also be your responsibility, for example, after an arduous crisis that may have depleted a good portion of your courage and stamina and tolerance, to make certain that your coffers are replenished and your inventory is ready again for the next challenge.

Another huge step forward is deciding exactly which values that you've chosen are *not negotiable*; things you cannot—will not—live without no matter what. I think you'll be amazed at how making one choice often clarifies a lot of other ones. Choices that you never imagined making a day or a month or a year ago.

For instance, suppose you discover while rearranging your inventory that quiet is something that seems oddly appealing, much to your surprise. You've always loved the craziness and noise of the city.

The thought of living in a peaceful setting never occurred to you until now. Yet you suddenly wonder, "maybe it's part of the reason I've been so stressed and irritable? And I know that being stressed and irritable contributed to the recent breakup with my girlfriend."

Well, maybe you're on to something! For in rethinking where and how you live, you may find yourself taking a path that leads to questions about a lot of other things so ordinary that they seemed, until now, set in stone and indelible.

Nothing is indelible or unchangeable, just as no one is irreplaceable. And perhaps where and how you're living, in the simplest, most basic terms, has been having a negative and eroding impact on your ability to be a nice, reasonable, loving and lovable person.

Discovering and digesting that one seemingly small shift can be an immense, mind-altering jumping-off point for you in considering new choices and directions you could take to be more satisfied and content.

Quiet. A simple but all-too-rare value today in this hyped-up, congested world. A quality of life that takes seeking and protecting to find and keep. And suddenly, quiet becomes a must-have, needed value to achieve.

Once you've made this kind of elemental leap, then you can move on to other values that would be nice to have but

Playing with a Full Deck™ No. 2 Worksheet

aren't do-or-die. Things like a small place in a quiet town near great restaurants.

Which is going to matter most? The quiet? Or the food? If you have to make a choice, which will it be?

For instance, you've now realized that you need a few basic things, such as quiet, clean air and space in order to not only feel more comfortable and content in your everyday life, but to also guarantee that you won't get another ulcer like you did last year.

You now know that you have too much stress and tension in your life and in your work as an editor for your well-being and peace of mind. Yet you live in the heart of a dirty, noisy city in a high rise apartment. And you work in a high-profile firm where deadlines are endless and tempers run high.

Do you really have choices? Can you afford to make a change? Now it's time to ask yourself one of the really tough questions: can you afford *not* to make a change? Has the price you're paying for the life you're leading finally exceeded the benefits?

Once you answer that question, it will feel like you're moving down a snowy slope, tobogganing towards the bottom. The further you travel, the faster you'll fly; ever easier, ever more exhilarated by the ride. And what fun!

Find one piece to this puzzle and a number of others will fall into place, as if by magic. All it takes is a dose of blinding truth and imagination to allow it to begin.

You'll make changes when you've reached break-point. When your status quo is suddenly so painful, so intolerable, so unbearable, that you will, you must, do something, anything. And when you've reached that place where you're willing to pay any price in order to resolve things and move on, you'll be standing full-tilt on The Inner Bottom Line.

Now that you've identified and clarified the values you cherish as well as new aspects of yourself, you might find it exciting and eye-opening to fill out another Getting Down to The Bone worksheet.

Please fill out
Getting Down to The Bone™ No. 2. Worksheet (p. 84)

When completed, review the first "Bone" worksheet that you filled out and compare your answers with this later version to see what changes may have occurred in your perspective.

You will find that when your perspective shifts, things suddenly take on a whole new look and meaning, and everything else shifts, too. Once clarified, it's easier to sort out those issues that are still acceptable and those which are *priced to go now*!

And that's when you'll draw the line and pay the price, whatever it takes, to change the status quo and have something you value and cherish more: peace of mind, resolu-

Getting Down To The Bone™ No. 2 Worksheet

Apparent Issue:
(Attached Emotions)

Underlying Issue:
(Attached Emotions:)

Source:

Duration:

Severity:

Options: Consequences:

Time Frame:

Solution:
(Attached Emotions:)

tion, freedom, respect, honesty, fairness, integrity. The list goes on, ad infinitum.

So let your mind run free. Take this adventurous journey of discovery. You might meet yourself along the way.

Setting Boundaries

Now that you've identified and organized what you're made of and what you value most, you're now ready to understand where you fit into the overall scheme of things in the world around you. How to protect and respect yourself and what you value most. How your ethics and values impact your everyday world. And, most importantly, what's in it for you. Because unless you're vested in it, unless there's something in it for you, it won't mean a thing.

Boundaries

Boundaries represent an integral part of the use and management of power, control and fear. Boundaries defend, protect and proclaim the existence of those things that are most valuable and honored by you.

With a clear understanding of boundaries and when, how, where and why to draw and respect them, you'll be ready and able to preserve the values you cherish most in yourself and in others.

Too few children are taught about the existence and importance of these invisible yet tangible borders because far too few adults truly understand, value and respect them. Yet once discovered and mastered, that awareness allows everything to shift and change into a much more manageable, sensible and orderly existence.

Consider, HJ, a mother and BJ, her daughter, who jointly asked me for help with a fascinating, ongoing dilemma that had reached breakpoint. Parent and child were battling over the age-old issues of boundaries, respect and trust.

The daughter, BJ, sixteen and a B student, had always tried to follow her parent's rules. But her mom, HJ, had been coming into her room whenever she wanted to whether BJ was home or not. HJ believed that her daughter's room was not off limits and as long as her child lived in their house, it was her right to do so. BJ felt it was an invasion of her privacy.

Last week BJ got so mad she got mouthy with her mom. HJ in turn became furious with her daughter and they had their first big fight, leaving them both upset. They were wrestling with a number of questions. Did this concern ethics? Was the daughter wrong to think she had a right to her privacy? What could they do so they wouldn't fight anymore?

I was impressed that they had chosen to deal with this disagreement in this collaborative way. It demonstrated an unusual and refreshing level of cooperation, quality and forthrightness in their relationship.

Initially, I focused on BJ's issues since it was her "turf" that was up for grabs. I assured her that she was not alone in her frustration, given the number of requests for help that I receive regularly from other teenagers also wrestling with trying to set or have appropriate boundaries, especially at home, and deal with this essential and often painful part of growing up. BJ was, however, uncommonly fortunate to have a parent open and willing to consider both sides and seek a solution acceptable to them both.

As to whether this dilemma involved ethics? Anything that involves respect, fairness and honesty involves ethics. And was BJ wrong or out of line to demand or need respect for her private boundaries? Absolutely not!

In order to establish a growing sense of self-esteem and respect, it was essential for BJ to feel trusted and honored in her home, particularly by her mother, the most influential and powerful female figure in her life right now.

However, that trust had to be fairly earned and maintained. So, as with so many issues, answers were conditional. For instance, if her behavior suddenly changed and began to create suspicion or concern that her well being or safety was being endangered, it would be understandable and appropriate for her mother to step in and take any number of preventative measures to protect her daughter. If that included searching a bedroom or bathroom, that might be the only way to learn the truth.

Parenting is not an easy job and this can be one of the toughest aspects of that responsibility. But, in BJ's case, since she was doing well in school and showed respect for her parents' rules, it didn't appear at this time that her behavior or conduct merited that kind of intervention or intrusion.

At sixteen, it was more than age-appropriate for BJ to want to take over more of the decision-making responsibilities and management of her own personal privacy than she has had in the past.

Respect for personal privacy and boundaries is built upon trust, and they would both benefit from some in-depth conversations about their personal definitions of trust, privacy, identity, respect and acceptance. The benefits and results from these dialogues could be astounding and invaluable.

As for HJ's responsibilities and role in this dilemma? There is one key issue present in this dilemma that mothers need to continually acknowledge and accept in order to help daughters grow into mature, productive and secure women.

Young women must learn how to create and design their own unique identities apart from their mothers' if they are to grow into healthy, separate people. The best lessons in life are learned from mistakes, not successes.

We all make mistakes. And no one can save us from making them. But in order to learn how to set and hold boundaries out in the big, bad world, we must first learn to do it and practice it at home where it's safe. Providing this safety was an invaluable gift that HJ could give to her daughter.

BJ also needed to understand that ethics was a two-way street. Just as she demanded respect for her private space and burgeoning value system, HJ also deserved respect for her rules and values.

It's not what we say; it's often how we say it that can make a difference. And while it's normal and human to lose our tempers, say things we don't mean and get really angry, it's also important to learn how to manage that anger and to find safe ways to cool off before trying to sort out issues.

It's also critical to learn how to respect differences and agree to disagree. Something they both were apparently trying to do really well.

As for the ultimate boundary, the one BJ owned around her private space? Her mom needed to accept that as long as BJ's behavior, attitude and actions remained respectful and admirable, she had earned the right to her privacy, and that they should take every opportunity they could to hug each other tightly, love each other well, and cherish what they have together.

Your Boundaries & Theirs

There are two kinds of boundaries that apply on The Inner Bottom Line. Your boundaries. And the boundaries of others.

There are also two ways in which boundaries are violated. Yours can be invaded. Or you can cross those that belong to others.

So how do they work? How do we know where boundaries exist and what we're supposed to do with them once we know where they are?

Let's first consider where boundaries are found and how essential it is that we acknowledge and respect them at all times.

There is a sacred, inviolate boundary around each and every relationship you have. While most relationships involve two individuals connected in some particular way to one another, a number of relationships involve more than two people, such as an immediate family unit, an extended family circle, a string quartet, a baseball team, or a group of colleagues as diverse as a rock band or an executive board.

There is one rule, however, that applies to all groupings. It is inappropriate and disrespectful, thus unethical, to reveal or talk about any conversation, revelation, plan or happening that occurs within that relationship to anyone who is not a part of the group. And, to make it even more complex, within each group there are primary relationships between each duo that must be respected in the same manner.

Just because you're on the same team does not mean that a conversation that takes place between the coach and the quarterback should be shared with anyone else unless both agree that is would be beneficial to the team to do so.

Simply stated, whatever goes on between you and someone else must stay between the two of you. Period. No exceptions. No matter what the size of the overall group or the importance of the information. (*There are, of course, exceptions to confidentiality, such as incest, abuse, or criminal activity.*)

Crossing Boundaries

For instance, you're the mother of two sons. You have an intimate, private relationship with each one. They, in turn, have a sacred boundary around the relationship they have with one another.

One day, during a phone conversation with your younger son, with whom you're very close and to whom you talk often, you ask him if he's heard from his older brother in the past few days. You go on to explain that you had left a message on the weekend but since you hadn't heard back from him, you didn't know if he was out of town or not feeling well. Your son answers yes, we actually spoke yesterday and he's fine.

Now. Here's where things can get dicey. You can choose to accept what you've been told at face value, respond with an appropriate, casual, "oh, that's good," and go on to something else.

Or. You can choose to cross a boundary where you don't belong and move into treacherous and inappropriate territory by doing a number of things. For example, you could ask him what they talked about, or ask what your older son is doing. Or perhaps if he's dating anyone new. (*Ouch, mom!!*)

You could even ask (*if you're feeling insecure enough to take the fact that he didn't call you back personally*) if there's some reason why he didn't return your call. (*Double ouch plus a really awful no-no!!*)

While you are free (*though perhaps not always wise*) to ask your older son those questions directly, it is inappropriate to try and triangulate your two sons by asking for information from them in this round-about way.

This area is often the most transgressed one during or right after a divorce, particularly when children are involved. Parents, despite their best intentions, usually end up zigzagging across major boundaries, leaving children caught up in their wake and in the middle.

There are other areas of communication today that are breeding grounds for crossed boundaries and invasive and abusive behavior.

Email is one of the biggest offenders. Not only is spam a complete and offensive violation of personal boundaries, but there are still no clear rules of etiquette and politeness regarding the sending and receipt of general messages, even between friends who manage very well in all the other areas of their relationship.

One of the most abusive aspects of electronic messages is the sending of group emails. This practice can become a dangerous and abusive invasion of privacy. For example, if, in sending out a message, you mindlessly list multiple addresses on it, particularly of people who do not know one another, and include anyone who has not specifically given you permission to give out their email address, you invade their privacy and boundaries, divulge private information inappropriately and possibly place them at risk.

Look at it this way. If you received a letter from me, would you turn around and include my address along with yours and perhaps ten other friends' addresses in the left hand corner of the envelope when you wrote a note to your buddy in Atlanta? I don't think so! Then why would you feel it's all right to do the same thing in an email? This invasive practice has created horrific security problems for millions of unsuspecting people. So if you have been doing this, please, stop it!

Gossip is another virulent form of boundary crossing and abuse. No one has the right to speak for or about another or on their behalf unless specifically requested to do so by that person.

It may seem that your comments are harmless and insignificant, but they're not. In order to be accountable and responsible, what is shared, spoken or considered between two people must remain between those two people unless both agree to share it elsewhere.

Respecting other people's boundaries sometimes proves to be too bothersome for some. They have a hard time accepting this concept, for to do so implies a willingness to accept differences without judgment or condescension. When confronted with a polite request to stop a certain behavior in the future, they might counter with, "you've got too many rules."

People unwilling to respect the boundaries of others without getting angry or resentful at being asked to do so often rationalize their superior attitude by claiming that it's just too complicated or demanding to know where boundaries are or how to keep track of them. They, of course, end up making it all about you, when it's really about them.

That kind of unwillingness to accept and respect another's needs that have been expressed politely and respectfully indicates an insecure person who simply can't accept your differences without needing to make you feel inferior or lacking. Certainly not the kind of relationship that would be good for you moving forward.

So take a look at the relationships and people around you. Whenever you find yourself part of or privy to someone who has the need to gossip or speak inappropriately, ask yourself why they do that. Why does anyone have the need to say intimate, personal, pejorative, unkind, even false things about someone else, especially when that person isn't there to speak for or defend themselves? Is that really behavior you want to participate in or encourage?

Drawing the Line

Now that we've looked at how you could violate or compromise other relationships, let's take a look at what happens when your boundaries are crossed.

You already know that whenever you feel uncomfortable in any situation for any reason, somewhere, someone or something is crossing one of your boundaries without your permission.

It can be as subtle as a casual conversation in which someone makes an assumption that is offensive, untrue or pejorative. For example, you're dining out with a few friends, one of whom brought along a man you've never met. During dinner, this man has one-too-many and is now running off at the mouth a bit loudly, much to the dismay of everyone at the table including the woman who invited him along.

Suddenly, he turns to you and says, "Hey, gorgeous, how 'bout you coming over here and warming up my lap?" Oops! Major crossing. Lots of choices here, from slowly pouring a drink in his lap as you sweetly coo that you're just doing your part to "cool him off" to just saying nothing (*sometimes silence can be eloquent as well as golden*), excusing yourself and leaving.

In another example, an old friend, who knows that while you have a great sense of fun and humor, you also have a lot of family responsibilities and can't just drop things at the spur of the moment, says in front of a group of others over lunch, "Oh, come on, join us tomorrow. The weekend will be a blast, unless you ruin it by being a party pooper again!" Ouch! Another yuck crossing. And what kind of real friend would say a thing like that anyway?

In the instance when a stranger crosses a boundary and behaves inappropriately, it's not acceptable but there's often some room for doubt as to intention and motive. But when someone who professes to be a friend or has known you for a while behaves in a disrespectful or unkind manner, that sort of crossing must be dealt with and can not be overlooked with excuses.

At stake, beyond the moment of insult, is the more important issue of the relationship itself and its value to you moving forward. It takes time to find out what someone else is made of and what kinds of values and ethics they are willing and able to honor and respect.

Taking care of yourself demands that you don't allow yourself to remain in any relationship with anyone who does not treat you with the respect, fairness and honor you deserve, no matter how old that relationship might be.

Additionally, it's equally important that they understand and know how to take care of their own boundaries, for they might be operating on the unspoken assumption that you'll do that for them. (*Don't do it!*)

The remaining key component to the adept management of boundaries is the awareness and sensitivity to know where they exist. And to completely respect and accept the fact that they are sacred and must remain inviolate.

Boundary Circles

Let's take a look at where boundaries circles are found, how they work and what behavior is appropriate within them.

We'll examine each circle briefly, starting with Circle A, the inner and most critical one.

Circle A is your Core Space. Each of us resides in this special, sacred space within which we grow and nurture our own Inner Bottom Line. It's a totally, private, intimate area where we experience and do things that are not appropriate to share with *anyone* else. And I strongly stress the word *anyone*. (*Use your imagination!*)

This space comes with one key, clearly marked *Do Not Duplicate*. This is the same key that we already discussed in Playing with a Full Deck.

As you will now probably admit to at least once in your life, you have, in a moment of passion or romantic ecstasy, made a duplicate key and given it to your intimate partner. You now also know that this action can be dangerous and unwise as well as disrespectful to yourself. This key is yours and yours alone.

You may invite your intimate partner into this space at any time of your choosing but it is inappropriate for them to move in permanently with all their possessions. This is the only truly private, sacred place you will ever own and control within which you are free to behave in any way that you need or choose to at any time.

Your intimate partner has their own Circle A and the boundaries of that space also deserve the same respect and protection as yours.

Circle B is your Private Intimate Space that is appropriate to share with your intimate partner as well as, during certain moments, with immediate family members. For instance, your bedroom is found in Circle B.

While it is appropriate for you to share that space with your intimate partner at any time, your children may cross that boundary and enter this space only during appropriate, special moments. For example, Sunday morning for a romp on the bed while you're reading the morning paper, or on your birthday or special occasion to bring you breakfast in bed. (*This is an area fraught with peril for all, including the dishes and floor. Use it wisely and keep a mop or vacuum nearby!*)

Circle C is your *Private Social Space*, such as the rest of your home and property, within which it is

 appropriate to invite extended family members, friends and colleagues to join you for private companionship, camaraderie, conversation and fun.

The space in Circle C has become more challenging today. The boundary that separates your home from your neighbors has been eroded by the inconsiderate, rude behavior of some who arrogantly believe that they can do whatever they choose to do at any time of day or night. After all, it's their house, isn't it?

While it may be true that they own their property and therefore, are free to behave as they wish within its walls, they also have a responsibility to be accountable for how that behavior or noise may spill over and impact those who live nearby.

Circle D represents what used to be known as the *Private Office*. It marks a space which is nearly extinct today, and its disappearance has introduced some serious and critical privacy and safety issues into our business culture.

It has been replaced by the open "landscape" cubicle that provides no privacy, no silence, and most of all, no safety.

Today's workers, often including management and executives, have no safe, appropriate place to deal with confrontation, anger, frustration, or even the simple, basic need for silence, solitude, respite or an occasional primal scream. With this space eradicated, we are forced far too often to handle inappropriate issues in front of or within earshot of others, sometimes to the humiliation and chagrin of all.

Circle E represents Company Space, the area within which most of us spend the majority of our waking hours during our lifetime. Today, within this space, there has also been a dramatic erosion of appropriate professional behavior that is often replaced with personal activities and actions that should remain private.

Circle F represents general Public Space and includes buildings, lobbies, hotels, restaurants, streets, sidewalks, parks, subways, airplanes, etc. This key area, along with Circle C, D & E, is being swiftly and terrifyingly eroded and destroyed.

Oddly enough, the same type of behavior is responsible for the destruction occurring in all of these areas. (*Anyone see a pattern here?*)

Please take a moment to review
the Boundary Circles worksheet. (p. 103)

Please note the solid circle surrounding Circle A denoting the importance of this boundary and the need for absolute respect.

Cell phones, wireless gadgets, boom boxes, and in general, rude, disrespectful behavior in public are quickly leveling boundaries that once were inviolate.

The misuse or abuse of public space concerns us all.

It has both distressed and sadly amused me to admit as a species that somehow over the ages we have developed and assumed an extraordinary, overblown arrogance that the earth and all that is offers belongs to us and us alone.

We seem to possess a selfish, distorted and ugly attitude that we are, in some way, its supreme ruler with an omnipotent right to plunder, pollute, and devastate the earth and its creatures as we choose. We act as predators rather than as polite guests. So wrong! And so scary!

Public space, which includes natural beauty, silence, and resources, belongs to itself, not to us. No matter how we

Boundary Circles Worksheet

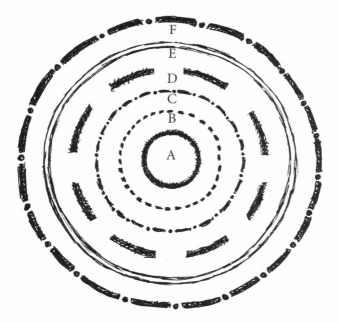

Private Power

A. Core Space
B. Private Intimate Space
C. Private Social Space

Public Power

D. Private Office
E. Company Space
F. General Public Space

rationalize it, no matter what books or legends or myths we weave, that is the natural order of the earth.

Just stand on the shore and watch a thirty-foot wave approach. Then tell me how big, god-like, dominating and powerful you think you are over Mother Earth and her awesome powers.

So to anyone who believes they can behave any way they choose in public, no matter how impolite, offensive, intrusive, disgusting or inappropriate that behavior may be, listen up! It's not OK!

You don't own any public space. No one does. And that includes the silence that existed long before any of us did. Therefore, you share in the responsibility to uphold a standard of conduct that is respectful and considerate of others at all times.

Whenever this issue comes up (*and it comes up much too much!*), I'm often reminded of one client, PN, who was so distressed and overwrought when he first came to me for help that I was concerned he'd have a stroke. Apparently he'd already been at breakpoint on this issue for a long time. Yet there is always one incident, even a small, seemingly insignificant one, that can send us right over the edge.

He'd put up with invasive, abusive public behavior on planes, in stores, in restaurants, even on the street. But a few weeks earlier, he and his wife had gone to the movies and in the middle of a very quiet, tense moment, someone's cell phone started ringing. To make matters worse, the phone's owner didn't turn it off or answer it right away. When he finally did, he talked so loudly it was impossible to hear the movie.

PN thought several people around him were going to strangle the man. After missing about five minutes of the dialogue, which ruined the movie for them as well as a number of other folks, he and his wife walked out.

The following day, however, the experience forced PN to consider his own behavior. He realized he'd been guilty at times of talking on his phone a bit too loudly in public, too.

He also felt angry and stressed from a growing sense of confusion over what was happening in general to the world today and questioned me as to whether or not I thought things were getting worse than they used to be.

PN's initial anger and distress were fueled by frustration, by a sense of being out of control and by an uncomfortable and embarrassed awareness of his own bad behavior.

Accountability is not always comfortable. We often react most strongly to qualities we see in others that we least admire in ourselves. But by acknowledging his own rude behavior, PN had told himself the truth and taken accountability for his part in the problem.

He had good reason to be angry. His evening was ruined. His boundaries were crossed. The entertainment he had paid for had been interrupted by a stranger too inconsiderate to act respectfully.

While this might sound like an insignificant, small, even trivial situation not worthy of mention, it is not trivial at all. Unfortunately, it happens all too often. It's an endemic situation in our culture and trying to confront it head-on can be very frustrating.

A majority of us have cell phones today. They can be invaluable aides for convenience, organization or, in an emergency, assistance. But they have also become an extension of our personal existence and a crutch for our needs. The problem isn't with using a cell phone. It's with misusing it inappropriately and talking loud enough so that every one within three feet can hear. That's not OK!

The person on the other end can hear us just fine if we speak in a discreet, low voice. Every day, while in a store, plaza or airport, my personal space is polluted by a person engaged in a loud, often personal conversation seemingly oblivious to anyone else and sometimes discussing things that would make a sailor blush.

I'm always tempted to ask what they're thinking but it's obvious they aren't. They certainly aren't thinking about anyone else. The choice to use a cell phone is like the choice between walking or driving. Before we had cars, we walked, whether ten blocks to the grocery or two miles to school. Once we had a choice, we opted for the convenience of riding and getting there faster.

Cell phones offer us the same instant option. Think of something to tell your honey? Why wait when you can call him while riding the bus? Who cares if your conversation is invading everyone else's ears?

And that seems to be the key point ignored by offenders. When someone behaves overtly in public, their actions spill over boundaries and into everyone else's space. Personal space is a odd, expanding and contracting concept: there is plenty of space around us when we're walking alone across a meadow, but we "pull it in" around us when we enter a crowded elevator.

There's a critical need in our lives for appropriate, courteous conduct no matter what we're doing. And that's what has been lost. While it's been eroding over time, things held together until the Sixties. Until then, it was unthinkable to do certain things in public.

There was an unwritten code of conduct upheld by people. They dressed to go out to dinner, travel, attend church or the theatre. Going out was a privilege and out of respect for that luxury, people put on their very best and generally behaved accordingly. And when they didn't, they were criticized, even ostracized.

But in the Sixties, when outrageous behavior was flaunted in order to inflame any authority figure as well as to "let it all hang out," it became anything goes. Now, we're assaulted within every dimension. And the lack of accountability for unacceptable behavior is the saddest part of it all.

Most of the appalling things I observe take place because someone acts out with an "if you don't like it, do something about it" attitude. Our culture is ruled by an arrogant in-your-face stance. It shows up on the screen, in music, in fashion, and in the graffiti defacing our public spaces. In the face of that, most of us retreat to silence or inaction rather than risk having our heads blown off.

I'm often asked if I think things are worse than they used to be; if we're slipping further into an immoral, unethical abyss. If viewed from afar, we haven't slipped much further than our ancestors who threw humans to the lions for fun. But I do believe we've been hurtling downwards for many decades and are still in free fall, headed who knows where.

So what can any of us do to prevent being caught up in abusive situations like these? Eliminating rude, outrageous public behavior, like eradicating litter or graffiti, can only be accomplished if each of us steps up to the plate and takes responsibility for our own actions.

Here's a simple but typical scenario. A stranger comes up to you in an airport lounge and asks you politely to please lower your voice, that he is having a difficult time reading with the level of your conversation. What would your reaction be? Chances are, if you're like most people today, you get pissed or really annoyed, say little or nothing and turn around and continue on the way you were, changing nothing.

In other words, you feel affronted by his demand, take it personally, become offended at his absurd request because, after all, you're doing nothing "wrong," refuse to take any responsibility for disturbing him, all the while mumbling to yourself that this guy is a real ass-hole! (*Familiar, anyone?*)

How else could this scenario have played out? How else could you have handled yourself without giving up some "sacred" turf you apparently felt belonged to you? (*An airport lounge? C'mon!*)

Perhaps the stranger was being unreasonable. Perhaps you had the right to feel a little bit affronted. But a simple, polite, "Of course. So sorry to have disturbed you," would have gone such a long way. And would have been an acceptance of whatever portion of responsibility belonged to you.

Everyone is a walking world. When someone asks you to be respectful or kind or considerate, even quiet, try to get outside yourself, *don't take it personally* and be empathetic rather than critical. They, too, have needs and rights and are asking for support. Give it. It won't cost you a lot and may bring you much more.

Responsible Power™. Such a simple concept. Yet seemingly beyond many people's willingness or ability to comprehend, for it is often just these kinds of complicated, emotional situations involving conflicting perspectives that stop us from knowing with certainty the best path to follow. And from doing the right and fair and respectful thing.

I'm often asked what the most ethical thing to do is in any given situation. Sometimes, it becomes a choice between two ethical values. And it can not only involve choices between ethical values, but also the integration of the responsible use of professional and personal power along with respect for boundaries, trust and loyalty. A veritable juggling act that is rarely simple, neat or easy and doesn't conform to formulaic behavior that you can phone in. Ever.

Take a look at the high-wire act NP had to perform while wrestling to amicably resolve a tough family and business dilemma.

He had found himself paying a very high price for his power and position. He ran a medium-sized company that was principally owned by his family and he had a lot of relatives working for him. That's how his father had run the company and NP was continuing that tradition.

He'd just learned after months of careful investigation that his brother-in-law had been embezzling funds. His brother-in-law had never been easy to talk to, had a quick temper, and NP couldn't say he'd been surprised by what the man had done. But NP was upset and at a loss as to the best way to handle this dilemma.

He hadn't been able to decide what to do, which was unusual for him and that had him even more upset. Should he just overlook it, which felt very compromising, make up the losses and not make waves, so that it didn't hurt his sister, whom he loved very much, or her marriage?

Or should NP confront the man and risk the possibility he'd leave the company and hurt other family members in his wake? Either way, NP felt he'd lose and it made him angry to admit that being boss was no fun.

You bet it's no fun. It's not unusual for people in this powerful position to be handed this kind of no-win situation I've dubbed the "no-choice choice." When the buck stops with you in every sense of the word, being boss is no fun at all.

And this treacherous situation is unique to family-owned businesses such as his and can become very complex and painful. One shift in the status quo can make everyone in the entire family feel involved, affected and entitled to weigh in with an opinion and that can be brutal for all!

NP had a lot on the line here and needed to cut himself some slack before forging out a solution. Since this situation, on one key level, was very personal, involving his relationship with his sister as well as his relationships with the rest of his family and his position as the leader of a family enterprise, he needed to be certain that he made choices from a position of objectivity.

There was also his relationship with himself. Not to mention his tenuous relationship with his sister's husband. That was a lot to balance and weigh and a lot of responsibility to carry.

When he and I first began working on this problem, NP was doing quite well in telling himself the truth, so that put him way ahead of the curve. And since the journey to that point is never easy or painless, he deserved kudos for that! (*Which he had forgotten to give to himself until I reminded him that they were way overdue!*)

He had also reached a point of clarity about several choices on the table: to cover up the incident and go on as if it hadn't happened, or to confront it and take responsibility for the outcome, which realistically, could have any number of unpleasant and costly consequences. Not easy choices to make.

Like so many choices in our lives, whichever one NP made wouldn't be neat and clean. Every action we take has an impact on others around us.

We stand together on common ground. Every time we yank a seemingly simple weed out of the ground, the roots left behind are intertwined somewhere deep under the earth with other roots and the pull is felt in some other plot of land nearby. Unfortunately, we often don't have control over where or when the tremor occurs!

There were a few possible scenarios that presented hard questions demanding answers. If NP chose to do nothing at all, how would he live with himself? How could he look himself and his sister in the eye in the future, much less his brother-in-law, knowing what he did?

What kind of price would he pay internally for carrying that burden? Would that be fair? Was it NP's to carry? And if he did nothing, what assurance did he have that it wouldn't happen again? Could he and the company really afford to have it happen again?

If he said nothing and covered things up, how would his brother-in-law deal with his wife and NP in the future, suspecting that they knew what he'd done but not certain if anyone one else did—for now?

In this first option, his deed would become the Sword of Damocles's, always hanging by a hair, threatening but never falling. It's what eventually drives criminals to turn themselves in, and the unfaithful to confess. It was a lot to carry and the burden would grow heavier, not lighter, with time.

Conversely, there was the fall-out from exposing the whole truth to everyone. Confronting his brother-in-law with his actions, possibly asking him to leave the company and work elsewhere, and even involving the law made this second option fraught with peril and consequence.

NP's brother-in-law was fortunate that he worked for a man who hadn't just picked up the phone, called the police and had him thrown out on his butt!

There was a third option that lay somewhere in between the ones already mentioned that might prove to be the most productive and manageable one given what was at stake for NP personally.

A starting point would be a private conversation with his brother-in-law, laying the truth out on the table with all of its positive and negative aspects, and letting him be a part of the decision, depending on his reaction.

He was an adult, and as such, was accountable for his actions. He should be held responsible for making amends by paying back the money as well as for making a commitment to seek help for his inappropriate and unethical behavior that had not only compromised viable business relationships but also many intimate ones along with the precious gift of trust.

By taking this position with him, NP would be making a clear statement that he was not now nor would he be in the future responsible for policing or monitoring him. It was his brother-in-law's responsibility to monitor himself.

The closing caveat with this option had to be: "You're getting another chance. But only one." In that way, NP would be drawing a crystal clear boundary for this man to honor.

If he ever crossed it again, he had been warned, in front, that all bets would be off. In that way, NP wouldn't have to be constantly looking over his shoulder. His brother-in-law would know where he stood with the company, with himself and with NP.

Choices between two ethical values. It can be mind-bending at times. Respect over honesty. Integrity over fairness.

In NP's case, he had a whole slew of combinations to consider. By choosing the final option, he was able to honor his innate sense of decency and honesty while still being brutally direct and frank with his brother-in-law. By doing so, he laid the responsibility for his actions squarely back on his brother-in-law's shoulders where it belonged and made him a part of the solution.

Responsible Power

As much as perception is reality, knowledge is power. Understanding and knowing what you're made of, where boundaries begin and end, and remaining in touch and aware of the impact you are having on the world around you gives you immense personal power and control.

Three Kinds of Power

I discovered this concept early in the work. I really owe my inspiration for it to all of the executives with whom I initially worked. It became evident to me, after consulting with the first few clients, that it was a concept I needed if I was going to improve their impact on others. Because what I first found was truly discouraging and upsetting.

There are three kinds of power: personal power—that is derived from who and what we are; professional power—that is derived from our position, status, or title; Responsible Power™—that comes from being accountable for the impact our words and actions have on others.

What I observed with these clients was a huge discrepancy between their use of power and control in one-on-one situations and the enormous change in their attitude, tone and visage as soon as they entered a company meeting, client's office, board room or walked in front of a camera or microphone.

Arrogance is a predictable offshoot of power. When you occupy a seat that demands attention, loyalty, obedience, even servitude from others who expect and accede control to you, it is understandable how easily arrogance can set in, sometimes without forethought or intention.

Too often, enormous power begins to instill a form of egocentric entitlement that seems to imply there is a separate rule book for those who possess it and that they really are their status, wealth or title. When someone reaches that level of arrogance and self-distortion, they are one step over the line into abusive power and greed.

I have often wondered, after a frustrating, too-taxing, private session with one of my CEO clients, whether or not they wear underwear made out of some other fabric than good old cotton, or breathe rarified air from a tube magically installed invisibly under their desks. Or what their conversations with their "God" must sound like. That is, assuming they (*still*) have one. Do they order him around too, just like everyone else in their life?

I've experienced examples of that kind of over-the-top power a few times in my music career. The first incident, in 1977, comes to mind whenever a discussion about the temptations of power arises.

I was being interviewed on the radio during a time when a new song of mine was getting a lot of airplay. I was talking with a really cool DJ out of Chicago on one of the strongest radio signals in the US. It was going well and we were both having fun.

In the middle of talking about the record, he asked me what I thought abut the present political mess in Washington. I remember so clearly the unexpected pause in the conversation (*we call it "dead air" in the business—it's a big "no-no"*), and my sudden awareness that millions of people were hanging onto the silence, listening to my every word.

And I consciously thought, "my God, this is power. I could say anything and they'd listen. And maybe even believe it!" Power can be heady, exciting, intoxicating and very, very distorting, because it's so easy to buy into it and believe that it's all about you.

Today, one of the most disturbing examples of abusive and destructive power emanates from celebrities who abuse their power and fame with the media to telegraph messages or behavior that makes negative, confusing or hateful statements to their fans, particularly adolescents.

The media also bears a fair share of the responsibility for this abuse by providing an outlet for these celebrities to reach the public. This isn't about censorship or free speech.

It's about appropriate and non-destructive behavior and messages. And about boundaries and choices.

I support and respect the rights of others to speak out on things they deeply care about. And I applaud those with fame and celebrity who do so in an appropriate and respectful manner, using their power to bring attention and much-needed resources to useful and valuable causes, issues and inequities. But the boundaries here are fraught with peril and must be continually examined and handled with great care, thoughtfulness and timing.

Even though I had something very intelligent to say to this DJ about the White House, it would have been inappropriate or unwise for me to misuse that forum and move from music into politics, just because I was suddenly given the power to do so.

That brief experience taught me, quite graphically, how easily power can be abused and how carefully choices must be made as to when and where and why we do what we choose to do.

Even if my intention had been pure and correct, if that had been misconstrued and not understood and seen as a publicity stunt rather than an honest statement as a citizen with First Amendment rights, it would have been a misguided decision on my part. For in the end, we all must be held accountable for our actions and words.

Power & Choice

But why? How does it work? What makes some people choose responsible power and others abuse. Is it always about control and accountability? And is it as simple as greed and profit?

To answer those questions, let's take a look at two kinds of power.

In the first scenario, you visit a shop to have your hair cut. You express politely what you want, you even bring a picture of your desired haircut, and then you wait patiently to have it done. Your hair is cut and it's not what you asked for. You say so but pay your bill in full, all the while receiving and giving acknowledgment that while it's not what you wanted, it looks good and you'll try living with it for a few days.

After a few days, you call back and ask that it be fixed, expressing your appreciation for the work done but reminding the hairdresser that it's not what you asked for in the first place. You are treated rudely and defensively, told that he's very busy and that it will be hard to find anytime at all to see you. And that even if you should decide to make the long drive to come in, there may be extra charges. Oh, brother! Sound familiar?

This is a common, everyday example of a small event in the grand scheme of life and yet, it's one of the most insidious, unethical and irresponsible kinds of abusive business practices.

In answering the ever-present question—what price are you paying for the life you lead today?—I'd have to rate this scenario at high cost.

Is it worth it? In this case, avoiding the insult and lack of courtesy is far more important and respectful of yourself than getting a great hair cut. There is always someone else to cut hair. You only have one Inner Bottom Line.

In the second scenario, you find yourself experiencing the Nordstrom way of doing business. You buy a pair of shoes. After a couple of weeks, you find you're not happy with them. The left toe pinches. They just don't feel comfortable.

You make a trip back to the store and express your unhappiness. And you're met with, "We'll be happy to replace the shoes with a different pair or give you a full refund. (*Here it comes . . . are you ready?*) What can we do to make you happy?" (*Oh! Sheer music to my ears!*)

Let's just change a few words in this scenario and it becomes an intimate, personal situation. A new romance. You meet across a crowded room and end up spending that night talking endlessly. Within days, you become inseparable.

After a couple of weeks, you find you're feeling a subtle sense of discord but nothing is said. You begin to discover that this wonderful person is lousy at communicating. They're not what you thought they would be or able to give or tell you what you need.

After much teeth gnashing and trepidation, with palms sweating and heart pounding, you take the ultimate risk, stand up for yourself and say so. And surprise of all surprises! You get Nordstrom in the bedroom! You're met with, "Honey, you mean a lot to me . . . what can I do to make you satisfied and happy?"

Boy, in either case, Door Number Two really works for me! How about you?

Every time I've found myself investing something I value, whether dollars or time or emotion, into something that treats me the way scenario number one did, it's a lost cause. I ultimately lose. Sooner or later, I'm going to find myself so stressed, so frustrated, so insulted, so disrespected or so overwhelmed that I have to end it, whatever the cost. (*And there always is one!*)

So what can you do? How can you know which kind of scenario it might turn out to be until you're in so far the cost will be high?

Well, first of all, you're only human. You can't always know. And if you don't realize it until it's a tad late, that doesn't imply that you're lacking anything essential or that you're stupid or insensitive. It just means you're human and that perhaps your "antenna" needs some refreshing or adjustment. We all have off days. (*Or weeks or years!*)

But. Pay attention. The signs are usually there in the beginning. Watch out if someone is overtly over-sensitive, defensive, subjective, critical, has erratic moods, gossips, and is temperamental, bitchy, unreasonable, paranoid, mean, unaware of appropriate boundaries, and complains incessantly. (*Anyone you now know?!*)

While this list may sound overdone, it's amazing how many troubled people use this modus operandi to manipulate their way through life exhibiting many of these traits. And we're nuts enough to put up with it! (*At least, for a while.*)

What can make a real difference for you, however, in the future, when confronted with any unknown situation, is to enter it very clarified about where your boundaries are, where you stand on your Inner Bottom Line, and what is simply *not negotiable*.

Rather than going through life adjusting to whatever gets thrown your way like a swaying reed at the edge of a pond, pick a spot, put down a few essential solid roots and remain grounded, no matter what happens.

When you know what you need and want in order to feel respected, honored and valued, choosing relationships and situations that are good for you becomes so much simpler and more fulfilling.

For instance, you're a talented fund-raiser with a background in non-profit organizations concerned with children's issues. You're offered a much higher-paying promotion to the national level that comes with a windowed office, perks and a lot of travel.

You know from several past positions you've held that you don't handle travel well. You have always found it highly stressful and lonely. You've also learned that it cuts into your ability to be as productive and useful as you need to be in order to feel good about yourself and your work.

On one hand, you would love to earn more money and have the chance to work at a national level; you've worked hard for this opportunity. On the other hand, however, you suspect that the requirements of the position, over the long haul, wouldn't be good for you.

You tell them you'd like a week to consider the offer. Then you hunker down on your Inner Bottom Line and try to sort out the temptations and glamour of the promotion from the hard truths. In your gut, you knew your answer the moment you heard the terms, but your head has been telling you to think it over, that you can do it, and that maybe this time is won't be so bad.

Crossroads. And time to draw the line. Do you sell yourself a bill of goods and overlook what you already intuit. Or do you face the fact that you just don't want to be on the road every week, all week long, away from your kids, your family, your home, even your bed. That the price you'll pay in stress and fatigue will outweigh any perk or ego-trip.

However, there's another interesting and valuable aspect to this dilemma that you mustn't overlook or devalue. You are not out of control or powerless. You have choices.

The organization obviously values your contribution and abilities enough to want to move you to the next level. Perhaps you can find a point of compromise that is good for you both.

Once you know what you will and will not negotiate, you are then in a much stronger position to open a discussion that will respect and honor your needs as well as theirs.

You agree to meet to discuss the offer. You come prepared to negotiate but not to bargain. You let them know respectfully that while you appreciate the opportunity as well as their acknowledgment of your value to the organization, you have a few guidelines that can't be compromised. The first and foremost one is the amount of travel. Can the amount of travel be amended to accommodate your requirements?

They may say yes. Or no. But no matter what the outcome is, you'll be able to accept it with a sense of security, professionalism, and pride that you were able to evaluate your needs and values, achieve clarity and peace of mind with yourself, and then assert your requirements in a manner that respected and honored your colleagues as well as yourself.

What makes this issue even more challenging is that for most of our "transactional" activities—buying retail, getting beauty services, making travel, resort or entertainment plans, etc.—we aren't around people long enough to see how they operate. And by the time we do see how they truly behave, we're usually mid-stream in receiving something we've paid for and it's too late. Where do you think the cliché "buyer beware" came from?

At the end of the day, after a positive or utterly infuriatingly disastrous encounter, always remember one thing: no one or no thing is irreplaceable. It's that simple.

No matter how much we tell ourselves that we can't survive without this person, or we won't be able to find someone to provide a unique and exceptional service for us, that's hogwash. It's simply not true. As long as we acknowledge we may have to pay a price to find a replacement to fill our need, we can always find an alternative resource.

Lost Boundaries

Where Were You When . . . ?

On September 11, 2001, every American lost something they will never regain.

During the months that followed, countless letters arrived from readers who were and still are struggling with emotions ranging from shock, terror and bewilderment to rage, revenge and intense grief.

Sadly, some of us lost more that day than others. But we all lost something in common. Our sense of living in safe harbor, protected, beyond reach, untouchable.

We have endured unspeakable carnage before, from the Revolution through the Civil War and on into this century with obscenities like Selma and Oklahoma City and Waco and Columbine. But this was different. The scope of it, the magnitude of it, was different.

Never before had our entire nation been subjected to a unilateral loss of security and privacy in one swift moment. Now, our new reality contained long lines at airport security, endless searches, document scrutiny, and increased profiling. Suddenly planes, trains and subways, always thought of as mindless conveniences to get us where we wanted to go as quickly as possible, became threatening coffins offering us, if we took the risk and boarded, a chance to play Russian roulette with a faceless man sitting in 26C.

I am certain that no American will ever forget where they were that terrible morning, for there are moments in life that are recalled not by "do you remember when?" but by "where were you when you heard?"

September 11, 2001 was just such a morning for me, much like the day John F. Kennedy was assassinated or Martin Luther King was murdered.

Until then, few moments in my life had left me speechless. Yet that morning, as I watched in horror as terror slammed into the heart of my country, no voice emerged to quiet my own nightmare, much less comfort those I loved. I had no answer why. I could think of no rationale or explanation to console or ameliorate the pain or fear that I saw on every face.

All I could do was listen, anesthetized by the endless flicker of the television screen and strangely soothed by Peter Jennings's gentle intelligence trying to help me make some sense out of senselessness.

At that moment, there was no thought to write anything. Good god, no! The whole idea of ethical choice, of responsible power and moral consciousness, was left hanging in mid-air, just like me, suspended like a doll with stuffing half-gone and one eye missing.

To all the reports, to all the developments, I couldn't even respond internally with "Oh. I see." I couldn't see, couldn't think, couldn't feel. The bad B-movie of that plane disappearing into Tower Two of the World Trade Center kept replaying, even in my sleep.

When the questions and calls began, from readers, from friends, and most importantly, from my daughters and loved ones, the enormity as well as the fragility of the ethical dilemma we were all caught up in really hit home hard. So for days, I wandered around, slightly dazed, not wanting to talk or be around others, and not able to think. I just needed to be. Be quiet. Be sad. Be angry. But most of all, just be.

When every American awakened on September 12, 2001, they arose to a new reality. No longer able to assume their borders were impenetrable, they discovered that destruction had carved a path deeper and broader and more far-reaching than what met the visible eye.

Our hearts were stricken and our souls were numbed. Our heads were mindless and our senses couldn't take in what we saw and heard and felt. We had been virginal, untouched, safe. Now nothing was the same.

For days, it was as if the entire heartbeat of our nation converged and wafted upward from a smoking, hellish plot of land at the base of New York. It throbbed and glowed night and day, biding us to watch and wait; hypnotizing us with its horror.

And as more time passed and the twisted steel and soot turned hope into despair, we still sat and stared, hoping the numbers rescued would rise and those lost would shrink.

Rescue turned into recovery. Days became weeks and then months. Tears and grief and lamentation turned to stricken, stoic acceptance and we all went on. But nothing was the same.

For myself, as time moved forward and my country's position began to be articulated in familiar yet strangely new terms, my irrepressible optimism began to shout out against my numbness and tears.

"Look! it proclaimed. "Out of unspeakable horror there's a glimmer of hope, a shudder of promise."

"Listen!" it yelled, "This is no longer a contest between nations; the line being drawn is just like The Inner Bottom Line! Now it's about values. About beliefs and morality. About civilization and barbarism. Maybe there's real hope for the first time. Maybe some good will really come out of all this evil."

Maybe. Then there was silence again and I was left in the stillness, pondering, waiting.

With each new morning, the unconscious movements of life—brushing teeth, making coffee, getting dressed, reading the mail—began to propel me into a semblance of normalcy and routine. And all the jumbled thoughts and feelings that had been racing around in my head began to take sides and argue amongst themselves. Right or wrong. Good or evil. Moral or obscene. Respect, fairness, honesty, integrity. Only four words, four values. Ethics summed up like a shopping list.

Late one evening, my oldest daughter called and spoke to me at length about her own personal conflict and pain in the face of these atrocities. Both of my grown daughters are strongly opposed to war and killing—for any reason. And oh, how I respect their values and ethics.

As she continued to talk, remembering the pride she had felt at being an American while spending three months volunteering in Africa in The Gambia, she had grown very emotional, reflecting on how privileged she was to live in this country and have such freedom and opportunity. Yet she opposed going to war and killing. It wasn't an answer to anything.

I had remained silent. Then, in the stillness, she had asked me if women were ever drafted, would I go? I had paused, thinking how strange and old, how generational I felt to have my own child, born in the heart of the 60's, ask me this dusty but familiar question.

And then I had realized that there was no issue, no dilemma, here. Not really. At least not for me. We all know what's right and good, moral and fair. Doing it is a whole other matter. And while we can argue over the correct prescription, no one disagrees about the sickness. It's not about being right or fair. Nor about being honest or moral.

No, it's much more than that. Being attacked changed all of that. So I had answered my child's question with this simple thought. "Doesn't the privilege of pride carry with it the responsibility of protection?"

And with refreshed clarity, I knew then that I would do whatever I could to help my country prevail. For if I'm going to enjoy the privilege of being an American, and all that provides—the inestimable freedom, the endless choices, the opportunities as well as the sense of security—then isn't my part of the deal to stand up and protect Lady Liberty when someone tries to blow her skirts off?

A few days later that galvanized sense of patriotism sat me down to face another empty page. I'd always known, without exception, that if someone threatened either of my children, I would throw myself in front of them without thought or hesitation. But now, it had sort of come to that in an unexpected way.

For wasn't that where we were? Wasn't the bottom line question: "What were we willing to die for? What did we cherish enough to give our lives to sustain?"

In the end it came down to the one ethical value that is always the hardest to define or grasp. Integrity. A standard of behavior. And an unwillingness to allow abuse of any kind.

For each of us, September 11th offered a rare opportunity to discover just what comprised the fabric of our own personal integrity. Our personal statement about our beliefs, our fears and the list of those things and people we cherished most and would give our lives to protect so that they could continue to live on.

Taking Back Control of Your Life

What we had lost was a sacred boundary. The border around our sense of entitled safety as Americans. And this obscene, collateral damage left many of us feeling a devastating loss of control over our lives.

In times of crisis, ethics often go out the window. There isn't energy or time to justify not stealing a loaf of bread in order to feed our hungry children.

And so during times of crisis, when everything we are and all we hold dear is put on the line as negotiable, we're sorely tested to plant our feet and stand strong, no matter what.

Anytime you feel as if you have lost control of your life, that's when all the thought, planning, evaluating and stocking up on The Inner Bottom Line will become your lifeline to your integrity.

Many have justified horrific acts of greed, selfishness or abuse in the name of survival. Wars are fought, corporate battles waged and divorces unleashed wrecking untold lives in their path, all in the name of "there was no other choice."

There is no justification for abuse. Or dishonor or disrespect. Or avarice or crime. Or terrorism of any kind.

And one of the most terrifying aspects of the battles being waged in today's world is that they're being fought by those on opposing sides who are fanatically convinced that only they are "in the right."

Making ethical choices to protect and defend what you believe in and are willing to fight for in the end is never neat or pretty. It's not black and white, right or wrong, simple or complex.

No matter where you stand on the issue of war, I'm certain most of us would agree on several sad facts: war is devastating, war is horrific, and war is hell. No matter who "wins," we all lose something.

On September 11, 2001, we all lost our inviolate sense of security. Our unquestioned sense of confidence. And our complacent belief that we would always be safe within the borders of our great country.

On that Tuesday, on a day that had, until then, represented one of the most joyous personal moments of my life, the birth of my younger daughter, on that sunny, simple morning, those boundaries were destroyed forever.

The Inner Bottom Line is about personal policies. Personal tactics. Personal motives. And personal survival. We can't change what has happened. The past is gone. There is no tomorrow. On the last stroke of midnight, what we thought would be tomorrow always becomes today.

We only have the present within which to plan our course, make our choices and accept responsibility for our reality. And that seems to be where so much of our grief and confusion resides at this time. Countless people, from all walks of life, are wrestling with the same basic questions.

How to move forward? How to plan for a future that suddenly, unexpectedly, seems fuzzy? How to feel in control or take back control of your life when everything around you seems so out of control? How to feel heard when no one seems to want to listen?

Since 9/11, most of us have been living each day with bated breath, waiting for the next shoe to drop. Of course, that's the basic intention of any kind of intimidation, any form of manipulation or terrorism. To replace the peacefulness of certainty with the shakiness of insecurity. To invade the serenity of confidence with the chaos of doubt.

And recent events have created a huge sense of loss and grief in this country. An enormous sense of helplessness and mistrust. A loss of the ability to have power over our lives and our destinies.

That's enough to send any sane person running for cover and question everything they thought was so. But running for cover doesn't get the job done. It doesn't allow us to earn a living, raise our children or climb into bed each night satisfied with the day.

So what can we do? How can we take back control over that part of our lives that is ours to own?

The one step we must take if we are to find a way to peace of mind and lightness of heart in the future is to accept our reality. By accepting that we can't change things that have happened, we will be left free to responsibly use our power and control to manage and decide things that are still possible while continually moving forward.

And after that? What's the next step during a time of survival? Buried within our instinctive moral imperative to survive is the will and determination to do whatever it takes to accomplish that goal. If it's expedient to sacrifice what we cherish and believe in most in order to feed our families and put shelter over our heads, we will usually pick warmth and food over honesty or fairness.

Therefore, in this time of challenge, when the essence of our freedoms and our beliefs has been put on the line and tested, we're all going to have to dig a little deeper and become more clarified about what is not negotiable and what price we're not willing to pay for expediency.

It's an opportunity for us to take a quiet moment and re-evaluate just what we really do cherish and believe in most. What values and ethics we will stand by, protect and not abandon. For each of us, the list will be unique. But you now know that the list will be short.

For you now also understand why nothing is irreplaceable. In the end, we end up with ourselves and those values which are essential.

Just before the light goes out each night, it is our own personal tally, our personal balance sheet that stares us back in the face. It's the sum of our parts, the totality of our actions that we have to answer to ultimately. Even if no one else ever knows what we've said or done, we'll know. And that is enough.

In times of crisis, in times of war, countless people over thousands of years have found or re-discovered the power of faith, the power of belief, and the power of simplicity.

September 11, 2001 changed countless lives. Families have moved in search of a simpler, more grounded lifestyle within which to raise their children.

Couples have divorced, realizing that life is short and time too precious to waste on relationships not worth keeping.

People have changed jobs, returned to school, taken trips, built homes, and shifted priorities in an attempt to find and create more meaning in their days.

We can regain some sense of control in our lives at a time like this by redefining and strengthening our focus.

Our clarity. Our priorities. Our commitment. And our belief.

These are the qualities that will get us through, whatever must be faced. Along with patience, compassion, courage and calm.

We tend to spend more time lamenting or questing for what we don't have rather than appreciating what we do. We often focus more on what is wrong or bad rather than on what is right or good.

Americans have re-discovered and shown their amazing stamina and bravery throughout every crisis in our history until now. We will again.

For at times of survival, when hope is tarnished, The Inner Bottom Line will become the first and last line of defense in your life. The only safe, sane place where you can stand balanced and in total control with infinite choices about your life and heart and soul at your command.

No one can take that from you. No one can ever own it. And no one can ever change it.

Except you.

Use it wisely. You can make a difference. Care for yourself and the world around you with tolerance, appreciation, and responsibility. And remember that everyone is a walking world.

The path to the good life isn't easy. You have to want it badly. And you have to work for it. But in the end, compared to the price you'll have to pay to have the other kind of "good" life, the path is simple and worth every blister you might get along the way.

Choices. Options. Clarity. Power. Control. Decisions. Accountability. Serenity.

Bon voyage! Enjoy the journey.

Epilogue

When it was first suggested that I write an epilogue, I found myself pondering the task more than I usually do before facing an empty page. Somehow, the idea seemed artificial and irrelevant, and I felt some discomfort without understanding why.

Over the years, I've learned to trust my sense of completion as a writer. I know and often long for the exciting anxiety that begins when I sense that I am growing ripe but haven't found the opening line to a new work yet. And I've also experienced the blessed curse of finishing. One of Webster's definitions for epilogue is "a closing section added to a novel, play, etc., providing further comment, interpretation or information."

Thus, it feels quite intriguing, even comical to me, to attempt to write a closing for something that doesn't finish. For The Inner Bottom Line has no end. It is an infinite, private, sacred place that stretches beyond now or then. It is a foundation that expands and contracts as we meander through our lives and it's always present even if we cannot see it. It is tensile yet weightless, absolute yet invisible, tangible yet untouchable. And it is ours and ours alone. No one else can ever own it, bend it, tarnish it or diminish it. Only we can deny it, ignore it, insult it.

So as my mulling continued, I began to realize that my work in ethics and my unexpected discovery of The Inner Bottom Line, so unlike my career in music, had never been about me. It had always been about others, even when they were initially reluctant to listen or consider the possibilities I suggested.

And that led me to once again acknowledge, even admit, as I have for so many years in lectures and seminars, that I'm just trying to muddle through life like everyone else. All I really do is offer options and throw ideas up in the air with the hope that one of them might land on fertile ground and take root in the mind or heart of someone else.

While that may sound corny to some, it has been during those magical moments that I have felt I was receiving so much more than anything I could possibly give. The look on someone's face when they suddenly 'get it' is like sun breaking through a heavy sky. The smile and the nodding head, like the doggie on the dashboard, when someone realizes that everything is truly personal and that they have so much more power and control in shaping their life then they ever imagined they did is like Christmas Eve to me. And the confidence that can infuse a timid soul when they realize they can make good choices for themselves is almost as delicious as chocolate!

But as good as that return on investment of time and energy has been throughout the years, nothing could have prepared me for the more recent response to The Inner Bottom Line column since it began running in newspapers. While I had written it to kind acceptance and appreciation for a West Coast magazine for more than five years, I never anticipated the readiness and thirst in the general public for what I have to say now. Not only have people been enthusiastic, warm and verbal about their loyalty, likening the reading of the column to a Sunday morning ritual with their first cup of coffee, but they have also been immensely specific about what and why they like the work so much.

And that has taken me quite by surprise. Even the occasional, irrationally angry reader who finds it necessary to tear me personally from limb to limb, thus reflecting a hot button of their own that my words must have touched, attacks me with greatly descriptive language. Ironically, it is the detail, the specificity, of my answers and the practical options and choices I suggest to the everyday questions I answer that seems to be infiltrating people's hearts and thoughts most deeply.

And that response tells me something even more valuable: that people are aching for specifics and that they no longer trust the vague rhetoric they're being sold. No longer are they content with smoky generalities or promises that sound too good to be true. For we've lost a great deal more of what was left of our innocence in recent times. Again. And yet, despite all that, like the born-again virgin, we seem to be a people who become disillusioned and jaded and then turn full circle and awake, one bright sunny day, believing all over again.

It is to that sense of rebirth, that willingness to start afresh, that I dedicate this book and its promise of hope and possibility. It is the first of other stories, the beginning of additional chapters and yet undiscovered challenges waiting ahead. For the work is never done as long as life continues; there will always be new mysteries, dilemmas, aggravations and joys we will be asked to face and resolve. But through it all, The Inner Bottom Line will be right there, providing us with stability and inspiration to face, accept and resolve whatever comes.

Colophon

This book was designed by Bruce Taylor Hamilton, wiith illustrations by Johanna Becker-Black. It was printed and bound by the Michigan firm of Thomson-Shore on Dexter Offset Natural text paper and bound in Holliston Pearl Linen cloth. The text face is Minion, and the display font is Dolphin.